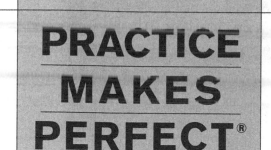

English Problem Solver

Ed Swick

New York   Chicago   San Francisco   Lisbon   London   Madrid   Mexico City
Milan   New Delhi   San Juan   Seoul   Singapore   Sydney   Toronto

1 2 3 4 5 6 7 8 9 10 11 12 13 14 15 QDB/QDB 1 0 9 8 7 6 5 4 3

ISBN   978-0-07-179124-3
MHID   0-07-179124-8

e-ISBN   978-0-07-179125-0
e-MHID   0-07-179125-6

Library of Congress Control Number 2012947472

Also by Ed Swick

English Verb Drills
English Verbs and Essentials of Grammar for ESL Learners
Practice Makes Perfect: English Grammar for ESL Learners
Practice Makes Perfect: English Pronouns and Prepositions
Practice Makes Perfect: English Sentence Builder
Writing Better English for ESL Learners

Contents

Preface

This book is aptly named a *problem solver*. Unlike other publications for learning English, it does not look at all aspects of grammar and structure; rather, it isolates those things in the language that non-natives often find complex or confusing. It then describes them, analyzes the complexities that cause confusion, and provides explanations and examples of how the problem areas work.

Most of the 20 chapters in the book delve into specific areas of difficulty. After these areas have been described, explained, and illustrated, they are put into practice in a wide variety of exercises; here, the reader can become more familiar with the problem areas, how they function, and how to take control of them. Some of the exercises require changing a word appropriately for the sentence in which it is found. Others ask the reader to insert a new word or phrase into a sentence. There are even a few multiple-choice exercises. In addition, most chapters have at least one exercise in which the reader writes original sentences. If a particular subject still seems difficult after a chapter has been completed, the reader should simply reread the chapter and practice the exercises again.

Homophones are a special problem for those learning English. Chapter 3 presents a variety of homophonic words and provides practice with them. But the list of homophones is quite long. Therefore, a detailed list is provided at the end of this book in the appendix. This resource will be essential for working with homophones.

The last chapter of the book does not discuss a specific problem area or describe any particular linguistic difficulty. Instead, it is a miniature linguistic laboratory that the reader can use to practice all aspects of the language simultaneously. Like any language, English is not a random series of conjugations, case varieties, and vocabulary. It is a combination of all those things that make communication in the language comprehensible and accurate. Therefore, the last chapter asks the reader to write creatively and not just practice with isolated concepts. The exercises are not for grammatical or vocabulary practice but a forum for the reader to apply his or her knowledge of English in a personal way. Of course, there will be some guidelines for this type of creative writing, but generally the reader will have ample opportunities to experiment.

This series of books is intentionally called *Practice Makes Perfect,* for that idea is basic to learning and mastering a new language.

Definite versus indefinite articles

Some native languages other than English do not use definite and indefinite articles. Therefore, speakers of these languages often have difficulty learning and using the English definite and indefinite articles accurately. This chapter will help to alleviate this problem.

Definite articles

The definite article in English is **the**. It is pronounced as **thə** (ə = schwa) when it precedes words that begin with a consonant.

> **thə** book
> **thə** funny story
> **thə** long book
> **thə** silly clown
> **thə** suggested material

But when **the** precedes a word that begins with a vowel, **the** is pronounced more like **thee**.

> **thee** apple
> **thee** eleven parts of the book
> **thee** interesting articles
> **thee** obvious results
> **thee** understanding

Remember that for some English words beginning with **h**, that letter is pronounced with an aspiration. In other English words, the **h** is silent. This difference will determine the pronunciation of the definite article. For example:

> **thə** *hat*
> **thee** *heir*

1

EXERCISE

1·1

Circle the correct pronunciation of the definite article **the** *with each of the words or phrases provided.*

1. little children — (thə) thee
2. amazing feats of strength — thə (thee)
3. evil empire — thə (thee)
4. local newspapers — (thə) thee
5. hours we work — thə (thee)
6. president — (thə) thee
7. residents of the hotel — (thə) thee
8. habits of whales — (thə) thee
9. newest automobiles — (thə) thee
10. advantage — thə (thee)
11. islands of Hawaii — thə (thee)
12. tall chimney — (thə) thee
13. honorary degree — (thə) thee
14. opinion of our readers — thə (thee)
15. liquidation sale — (thə) thee
16. heavy burden — thə (thee)
17. latest news — (thə) thee
18. unbelievable story — thə (thee)
19. yellow bird — thə (thee)
20. eventual outcome — thə (thee)

The definite article is used to modify a noun that is *the specific subject* of a speaker or writer. It is a person or thing that is *known and being discussed*. For example:

The man on the corner is my friend.

In this sentence, **the man** is the specific subject of the speaker. He is also known to the speaker, because he is a friend. Let's look at another example.

I know **the answer** to this question.

In this sentence, **the answer** is the specific subject of the speaker. It is the thing that is *known and being discussed* by the speaker. Let's look at one more example.

> We keep our car in **the garage**.

Here, **the garage** is the specific location where our car is kept. It is a known place and is our subject.

EXERCISE
1·2

In the blank provided, write the phrase that is the specific and known subject of the writer of the sentence. If there is more than one, write all of them. For example:

John didn't like the blue suit and returned it.

the blue suit

1. Our family needs a vacation and will travel to the state of Florida for some sunshine.

   the state of Florida

2. The problem in a business is always the lack of customers.

   the lack ; the problem

3. I want to take the children to the park.

   the children , the park

4. Did the tour guide find a beach for the tourists?

   the tourists ; tour guide

5. The boys refused to play with the girls.

   the girls ; the boys

6. She needs a lamp for the guest room.

   the guest room

7. The newspaper was lying on the porch in the pouring rain.

   the porch ; the newspaper

8. Let me know whether you find an article about the war.

   the war

9. The scholarship winner wants to attend a university in the East.

   the East ; the scholarship

10. Who made a hole in the wall?

    the wall

Indefinite articles

The English indefinite articles are **a** and **an**. Use **a** before a word that begins with a consonant and **an** before a word that begins with a vowel.

> **a** long story
>
> **a** pleasant surprise
>
> **a** stranger
>
> **an** anteater
>
> **an** exciting movie
>
> **an** orchestral piece

A word of caution regarding vowels: The vowel **u** is sometimes pronounced as **yoo**. In such cases, it is preceded by **a**.

> **a** university

EXERCISE
1·3

*Write the correct indefinite article, **a** or **an**, in the blank provided.*

1. _____an_____ apple

2. _____an_____ angry man

3. _____a_____ crazy tale

4. _____a_____ laughing boy

5. _____a_____ unique story

6. _____a_____ history lesson

7. _____a_____ casual remark

8. _____a_____ zookeeper

9. _____an_____ yawning baby

10. _an_ ~~an~~ understandable mistake

11. _____an_____ insult

12. _____an_____ opening to the play

13. _____a_____ tragic end

14. _____a_____ universal remote

15. _a_ ~~an~~ cell phone

16. _____an_____ Internet connection

A e i o u y
when u - yoo,
then a

17. *an* entertaining program

18. *an* ugly duckling

19. *a* honorable peace — ?

20. *an* ordinary day

Indefinite articles modify nouns that are not the specific subject of a speaker or writer. Such nouns are considered *generalities*. The word *any* can often replace the indefinite article and make sense. This is usually the signal that the indefinite article is the preferred choice over the definite article. For example:

Do you have **a book**? (Do you have *any* book? Do you have *any* books *in general*?)

The person asking this question is not looking for a specific book but rather *any* book that might be available.

There is **a strange man** on the corner.

The man in this sentence is not known to the speaker. Thus, he is not the known subject of conversation. The speaker is probably wondering who the stranger is.

When a nonspecific noun is introduced, it is most often modified by **a** or **an**. But once it has been introduced, it becomes specific and can be modified by **the**. It is the known subject of the conversation. Consider the following dialogue:

Toм: There is **a** strange man on the corner. Do you know him?

Mary: I have never seen **the** man before.

Toм: I think **the** man might be lost.

Mary: Perhaps we should help **the** man.

Consider another example:

Toм: I want to buy **a** bike for my son. What kind should I get?

Mary: I like **the** red bike over there.

Toм: **The** red bike is really nice but a little big for my son.

Mary: **The** blue bike is a bit smaller. How about that one?

Notice that the addition of adjectives (**red** and **blue**) makes the bike more specific.

The choice of **a** or **an** and **the** is often a matter of intent. Does the speaker wish to suggest that a noun is being discussed generally (any person or object)? Or does the speaker wish to imply that a specific noun is the subject of the conversation (the known person or object)? For example:

I like a cold beer. (I like any glass of beer that is cold. Generally, I enjoy a cold beer.)

I like the cold beer. (I just tasted three beers. I only enjoyed one—specifically, the cold beer.)

*In the blanks provided, write the correct definite or indefinite article—**the**, **a**, or **an**.*

1. ___the___ story that ___the___ children are reading was written by ___the___ woman in England. But I don't remember her name.

2. Do you have ___a___ pencil I can borrow? I left my schoolbag on ___the___ kitchen table.

3. Did you enjoy ___the___ opera this evening? / Not really. I thought ___the___ baritone was weak and ___the___ orchestra too loud.

4. We just bought ___a~~the~~___ cottage in the woods. / What good news. I'd love to see ___the___ cottage some day.

5. I need ___a___ vacation. I've worked for ___the___ company for six years, and now I want a couple weeks by ___a___ lake or pond where I can fish.

6. Sometime next year, I want to spend ___a___ week hunting in Colorado. They say that ___the___ mountains are beautiful in ___the___ autumn. Perhaps I should go then.

7. My husband needs ___a___ new suitcase. Let's go to ___the___ mall on Main Street. There's supposed to be ___the~~a~~___ great leather goods store there.

8. Do you have ___an___ extra pen? I lost ___the___ one my brother gave me last year. I want to write him ___a___ letter and get it to ___the___ mailbox on ___the___ corner before 4 p.m.

9. There's ___a___ little boy alone in ___the___ park. He seems lost. / I think I know ___the___ boy. He lives in ___a~~the~~___ large, white house on ___the___ hill outside of town.

10. John bought me ___a___ bracelet yesterday. / What does ___the___ bracelet look like? / I'm not sure. I haven't seen ___the___ bracelet yet. John hid it somewhere in ___a~~the~~___ basement.

Plural articles

Definite and indefinite articles function not only in the singular but also in the plural. The plural indefinite article, however, is no article at all. The plural noun stands alone and implies a generality. If the word *any* can be used with the plural noun, it is indefinite. For example:

books	(books in general, any books)
nations	(nations in general, any nations)
children	(children in general, any children)

Compare the use of definite and indefinite articles in the singular and plural. Keep in mind what the difference of meaning is.

arpeg — the

DEFINITE ARTICLE	
SINGULAR	PLURAL
the house	the houses
the huge ship	the huge ships
the man	the men
the nervous horse	the nervous horses

heonp. arpille a an

INDEFINITE ARTICLE	
SINGULAR	PLURAL
an angry mob	angry mobs
an astronaut	astronauts
a mountain	mountains
a television program	television programs

Certain singular nouns that express something of a nonspecific nature or collectiveness can be written without an article. This structure implies a generality. For example:

Beauty is only skin-deep.

Time can be your enemy or your friend.

Money is the root of all evil.

Hard work can be a character builder.

EXERCISE
1·5

Rewrite each sentence by changing the underlined singular nouns to the plural. Make any other necessary changes to the sentences.

1. The boy played in the field with a dog.

   The boys played in the fields with dogs

2. We have a new gardener for the new nursery.

   We have new gardens for the new nurserys

3. When on a vacation in Hawaii, I often visit a young surfer at the beach. *young surfers*

   When vacations in Hawaii, I often visit at the beach

4. If you can find a racket, we can go to the tennis court and try to find a partner for you.

   If you can find rackets, we can go to the tennis corts and try find partners for you

5. The child never watches a movie of which the nanny does not approve.

The childrens never watches movies of which nannys

6. If I had a puppy, I would give the puppy to a lonely man or woman.

men or woman

If I had puppys I would give the puppys to lonely

7. The reason for my tardiness is simple: there was an accident on the snowy road, and the police officer halted all traffic.

road

the reasons for my accidents on the snowy

8. Put a candle on the table and a bottle of white wine in the cooler, so we can celebrate.

candles the tables bottles the coolers

9. Did you send the lawyer a telegram or an e-mail?

the lawyers telegrams of the e-mails

10. A pretty woman approached the car and held up a sign asking for help.

pretty woman the cars signs

EXERCISE
1·6

Rewrite each sentence by changing the underlined plural nouns to the singular.

1. The boys ran across the gardens and ruined rows of vegetables.

The boy the garden a row of vegetables

2. Rainstorms and windy days made the sightseeing trips miserable.

A rainstorm a windy day the sightseeing trip

3. The new students had to carry trays of milk cartons into classrooms.

The new student a tray a classroom

4. Are tourists from European countries better tippers than tourists from Asia?

a for

a the tourist an European canty a better

5. The reindeer bolted into the fields and startled the resting geese.

The r the field the

Circle the letter of the word or phrase that best completes each sentence.

1. Ellen wanted _____ but didn't know where to buy one.
   a. the green blouse   (b.) a new sweater   c. purchases   d. money

2. Who was _____ unusual-looking man I saw in town yesterday?
   a. a   (b. an)   c. the   d. any

3. John accepted _____ she made but was a bit skeptical.
   a. reasons   b. logic   c. the anger   (d.) the excuses

4. I'm looking for _____ interesting book to read on the plane.
   a. these   b. a   (c.) an   d. the

5. They were in _____ hour-long discussion about the new project.
   a. any   b. several   (c.) an   d. a frequently

Capitalization and punctuation

Capitalization

European languages all use capitalization as a way of highlighting certain kinds of vocabulary. English is no different. There was a time when capitalization in English was a bit easier, because the general rule was to capitalize all nouns. Look at the following excerpt from the US Constitution and notice that all the nouns are capitalized.

Article I—The Legislative Branch

Section 1—The Legislature

All legislative Powers herein granted shall be vested in a Congress of the United States, which shall consist of a Senate and House of Representatives.

Section 2—The House

The House of Representatives shall be composed of Members chosen every second Year by the People of the several States, and the Electors in each State shall have the Qualifications requisite for Electors of the most numerous Branch of the State Legislature.

No Person shall be a Representative who shall not have attained to the Age of twenty five Years, and been seven Years a Citizen of the United States, and who shall not, when elected, be an Inhabitant of that State in which he shall be chosen.

This simple approach to capitalization is, unfortunately, no longer in vogue. However, standard rules exist to guide accurate capitalization of English.

There is only one pronoun that is always capitalized: **I**. However, this occurs only in the subjective case. The objective cases of **me**, **my**, **mine**, and **myself** are not capitalized unless they occur at the beginning of a sentence.

Names

The simplest and perhaps most obvious rule of capitalization is that all names—first names, middle names, or surnames—are capitalized.

George Washington

Franklin Delano Roosevelt

Helen Keller

Martin Luther King Jr.

Titles

The titles that accompany names are also capitalized.

Dr. Jonas Salk
Mr. Brad Pitt
Ms. Gloria Steinem
President Barak Obama
Professor Maria Ibbotson
Queen Elizabeth II
Senator Dianne Feinstein

First word of a sentence

Always capitalize the first word of a sentence, whether the sentence is a statement, a question, or an exclamation.

My brother has a new job in New York City.
Have you ever visited Disneyland?
Watch out for that car!

EXERCISE
2·1

Rewrite each word that requires a capital letter.

1. during the late afternoon, i like to stroll down to the river and visit mr. smith.

   _D_ _____ _Mr Smith_

2. are frank and ellen coming to your party tomorrow?

   Frank Ellen _____

3. i bought a puppy yesterday and decided to call her spotty.

   _____ _Spotty_

4. why does professor keller continue to call me edward? my name is john.

   Professor _Edward_ _John_

5. dr. parsons said that this was the worst novel he ever read.

   Dr Parsons

6. don't just stand there! help me!

   _Me_

7. the newly elected president will take the oath of office tomorrow.

   President

8. we wanted to meet vice president biden, but he was much too busy.

_____ *Vice president* _____

9. last night, little mary began to cry, and when i went to her room, i realized she had had a nightmare.

_____ *Mary* _____

10. could you spend some time with mrs. martin? she's been rather lonely.

_____ *Mrs Martin* _____

Quotations

When sentences occur in *direct discourse* (a direct quote), the sentence that introduces the quote does not begin with a capital letter unless it is the first word in the sentence. For example:

> "**Be** careful!" Bob shouted. "**That** machine is dangerous!"
>
> "**I** see you hiding there," the man called to the children.
>
> She said, "**You** need to find a job soon."
>
> My aunt asked, "**Why** does that woman chase after you?"

Quotations do not occur in *indirect discourse*, which is the retelling of what someone has said. The quote does not begin with a capital letter unless it is a word that requires capitalization (such as **I** or a proper noun).

> Bob shouted that we should be careful, because that machine is dangerous.
>
> The man called to the children that he saw them hiding there.
>
> She said that I need to find a job soon.
>
> My aunt asked why that woman chases after me.

Places

Towns, cities, nations and nationalities, continents, regions, and all other proper nouns are capitalized. If the proper noun consists of more than one word, all the primary words are capitalized. For example:

> United States of America
>
> Africa
>
> Dade County
>
> San Francisco
>
> Brooklyn Bridge
>
> Princeton University
>
> St. Paul Lutheran School
>
> Art Institute of Chicago
>
> English

Titles not capitalized

It has already been explained that titles that precede a name are capitalized. But they do not always have to be capitalized. If they are used to identify a rank, they appear without a name and are not capitalized.

> The **king** came into the room.
> Mr. Barton was the last **senator** to enter the hall.
> Is Doris Whitman the new **principal** of the school?

But if you use a title to address a person, then it must be capitalized.

> Did you get the test results, **Doctor**?
> Please have a seat, **Senator**.
> I look forward to reading your book, **Professor**.

EXERCISE
2·2

Rewrite each word that requires a capital letter.

1. mr. president, have you been in touch with the government of iran?

_____

2. "please control yourselves," the young teacher pleaded.

_____

3. when the governor came into the room, senator smith stood to shake his hand.

_____

4. she asked whether the queen will spend some time at windsor castle.

_____

5. captain jones wrote, "i was shocked to see the russian ship floundering in the bering sea.

_____

6. did ms. keller have a chance to read the declaration of independence?

_____

7. my boss has to take a new job in either boston or philadelphia.

_____

8. my favorite actress is angelina jolie, whom I once saw in a hotel in california.

_____

9. the new museum is only a block from new york university.

_____

10. "turn down that music!" mr. brown bellowed. "i need some sleep before i fly to europe!"

_____

Books and periodicals

In titles of books and periodicals, do not capitalize prepositions. For example:

> The Last *of* the Mohicans
> Catcher *in* the Rye

In addition, the articles **the**, **a**, and **an** should not be capitalized unless they are the first word of the title. This is also true of the words **as**, **and**, **but**, **if**, **nor**, and **or**.

> A Raisin in the Sun
> Romeo and Juliet
> The Aspen Times

The verb **to be** and its conjugated forms (**am**, **are**, **is**, **was**, and **were**) should always be capitalized in titles.

> Be It Ever Thus
> Are We as Interesting as We Think We Are?

Compass points

When points on the compass refer to a specific region, they should be capitalized. But when they identify a direction or a location in general, they are not. For example:

> The **South** struggled in the last year of the Civil War.
> My brother lives in the **East** now, not far from New York City.
> I turned on the engine, put on some music, and headed **west**.
> The **northern** part of the state consists mostly of farms.

Seasons of the year

Do not capitalize the seasons of the year unless they are the first word in a sentence.

> **Spring** is probably my favorite time of year.
> We often spend the **summer** in Canada.
> **Winter** sports interested me a lot when I was young
> The **fall** colors are disappointing this year.

If a season occurs in a title, it should be capitalized.

My favorite song is "**Autumn** Leaves."

Rewrite each word that requires a capital letter.

1. my father reads *the new york times* every morning.

   _____

2. our library doesn't have *to kill a mockingbird* on its shelves.

   _____

3. the department of state issued a warning through an official statement.

   _____

4. *life on the mississippi* is considered a classic.

   _____

5. professor howard's new book, *the war against poverty*, is doing well.

   _____

6. the doctor spent a lot of time in a london museum to enjoy the works of gainsborough.

   _____

7. tony has spring fever and doesn't want to go to work.

   _____

8. mark and helen tried out for *our town*, but the director wasn't interested in them.

   _____

9. i sold my ford convertible and want to buy a cadillac.

   _____

10. the stories of cowboys and indians in the west are partly just myth.

    _____

School subjects

Do not capitalize the name of a school subject unless it is part of a specific course name. For example:

SUBJECT	COURSE NAME
history	The History of Europe
art	Renaissance Art
geometry	Principles of Geometry
foreign language	German I

Series

If two or more sentences follow a colon, each sentence should be capitalized. But if there is only one sentence or just a series not contained in a complete sentence, do not capitalize the first letter following the colon. For example:

> The parade was an outstanding success: Men proudly carried Old Glory. The crowds cheered and waved little flags above their heads.

> Thomas Kelly is a bright student: his essay on the Depression was excellent.

> As usual, Mom was prepared for the picnic: sandwiches of every type, a case of soft drinks, and a homemade apple pie.

EXERCISE
2·4

Rewrite each word that requires a capital letter.

1. i signed up for german but transferred to another language after one week.

   _____

2. michelangelo was more than a renaissance man: he was an inventor. he was an artist. and he was a visionary.

   _____

3. my sister hates math, but ms. butterworth is such a good teacher that she studies a lot.

   _____

4. we need fixings for sandwiches: cheese, sausage, mustard, and bread.

   _____

5. when we were in the midwest, we visited chicago and shopped on michigan avenue.

   _____

6. in economics, we read *a new theory of capitalism* by miriam thorn, economics professor at the university of toronto.

   _____

7. although i like the geography of the world, i found it of little use in my chemistry class.

   _____

8. most freshmen had certain required courses: english, algebra, introduction to computers, and two electives.

   _____

9. the young prince married his bride in westminster abbey on a beautiful saturday afternoon.

   _____

10. my professor has a subscription to *the wall street journal*.

   _____

Punctuation

The purpose of punctuation marks is to show in writing the inflections that occur in speech: the intonation of a question, an ordinary statement, powerful emotion, or even parenthetical ideas.

Period

Use a period at the end of a sentence that is not a question or an exclamation.

> Tomorrow is the fifth of January.
> I need to pay that bill by the end of the week.
> John tried to kiss Amy.

Use a period as a decimal point to set off a decimal amount or dollars from cents.

> Nearly 5.75 gallons of fresh water are needed.
> How much is 3.1 + 8.25?
> That accident cost me $545.85.

Periods are also used after initials.

> Have you read T. S. Elliot?
> This book is about John D. Rockefeller.
> She arrived at 8:00 a.m.

Use a period with abbreviations.

> I recently met Ms. Carson.
> Dr. Phillips isn't in today.
> Mary received her M.A. from Yale.

If a vertical list is numbered, each number is followed by a period.

Things to do today:

1. Go online to find the address of the store.

2. Stop at the bank to withdraw $300.

3. Shop carefully and look for sales.

Question mark

A question mark is used after a question. It can also be used following a declarative sentence to suggest disbelief in the statement and thereby making it an exclamation.

> How much did you pay for that puppy?
> May I have this dance?
> You bought an expensive luxury car?

Exclamation point

Use an exclamation point to make a strong statement or to show emotion.

> Look! That man fell out of the window!
> Shut up! Leave me alone!
> I love her so! I'll never get over her!

EXERCISE
2·5

In the blanks provided, supply the missing punctuation mark (period, question mark, or exclamation point) with the word or abbreviation provided in bold. For example:

I have never met **Mr** Jones. _Mr._

1. The train is supposed to arrive at 9:00 **pm** ___p.m___
2. Have you had a chance to read my **manuscript** ___?___
3. The little candle is only **2 5** inches long. ___2.5___
4. "Close that door right **now**" he shouted. ___!___
5. Why do you always arrive late to **work** ___?___
6. Watch **out** There's a truck coming around the **corner** ___!___ ___.___
7. Dad is out in the yard raking **leaves** ___.___
8. My brother finally got his **BS** degree. ___B.S.___
9. What kind of costume is that supposed to **be** ___?___
10. Get out of **here** ___!___
11. I miss my family so **much** ___!___
12. Be sure to read Chapter Ten before Monday's **class** ___.___
13. Are you sure you know how to get **there** ___?___
14. Today is Bill's **birthday** ___!___
15. That scarf costs **$15 99**. ___15.99___

Comma

When listing at least three items in a series, separate them with commas. If there are only two items in the series, use **and** instead of a comma. For example:

> Jean bought a loaf of bread, some bananas, and a pound of coffee.
> I need a new toothbrush and a bar of soap.
> After dinner I'm going to wash my hair, take a long shower, and then curl up with a good book.

Use a comma to separate the day from the year in a date.

> She was born March 5, 1999.
>
> His birthday is on June 21, 2010.
>
> Where were you on September 11, 2001?

When providing an address, separate the street from the town and the town from the state with a comma. Do not use a comma before a zip code, if one is included.

> My new address is 1400 N. Lincoln Road, Albany, New York.
>
> Do you still live at 1886 Benson Street, Chicago, Illinois 60600?

If a prepositional phrase or adverbial phrase introduces a sentence, a comma should be used following the phrase if it is rather long. For example:

> Yesterday I went to the gym to work out.
>
> During my last year in college, I met my future husband.
>
> While visiting relatives in Ireland, we spent two nights in an old castle.

If a sentence begins with a dependent clause, use a comma. But if the dependent clause comes at the end of the sentence, do not use a comma.

> When Jerry showed me her picture, I knew it was an old girlfriend of mine.
>
> If you follow the instructions, you'll have no trouble building the model.
>
> I'll be happy to help you if you find the problem too hard to solve.

A comma is used to separate every three digits in a long number. However, this approach to numbers is not used with years. For example:

> That bicycle costs $2,500.
>
> The population is now over 300,000,000.
>
> John Kennedy was elected president in 1960.

In a compound sentence, place a comma before the conjunction. If the sentences in the compound are short, the comma can be omitted.

> I hurried to the lecture hall, because Professor Smith always had something important to say.
>
> You still have fourteen math problems to do, so you'll have to burn the midnight oil tonight.
>
> Mary won and we cheered.

If a sentence is interrupted with parenthetical information, the interruption is set off with commas. For example:

> My boyfriend, as usual, was late.
>
> Your debts, of course, were caused by your need to shop.
>
> The meaning of this article, although somewhat vague, is criticism of the mayor.

If two or more adjectives modify a noun equally, they should be separated by commas.

> Jane loved the cute, little puppies.
> I need a big, cold beer!

Commas separate an interjection from the rest of the sentence.

> Well, I see you're late again.
> Oh, what a beautiful sunset.
> Ah, how cute your baby is.

In direct discourse, a comma is used after the phrase that introduces the quote.

> She asked, "Do you know the way to the library?"
> My father said, "Take the car and pick up Aunt Mary at the station."

If the quote is the first element in the sentence, question marks and exclamation points are used in place of a comma. If the quote ends with a period, a comma replaces it. For example:

> "Can you direct me to the subway?" the tourist asked.
> "Stop all that screaming!" he shouted at her.
> "I need a nice, long nap," she sighed.

Use a comma to separate the person addressed in a sentence.

> Uncle Bill, do you know the capital of Maryland?
> Children, take out your spelling books.
> That's no way to act, Tom.

Use a comma to separate an appositive from the rest of the sentence.

> Laura, my youngest sister, is in medical school right now.
> Richard Snyder, our new mayor, is only twenty-nine years old.
> They finally captured the thief, a boy of only eighteen.

In an informal letter, use a comma after the greeting and after the closing. For example:

> Dear Ms. Collins,
> Dear Uncle George and Aunt Louise,
> Sincerely yours,
> With love,

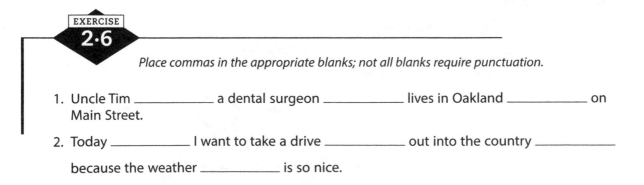

EXERCISE
2·6

Place commas in the appropriate blanks; not all blanks require punctuation.

1. Uncle Tim _____ a dental surgeon _____ lives in Oakland _____ on Main Street.

2. Today _____ I want to take a drive _____ out into the country _____ because the weather _____ is so nice.

3. During my first semester _____ , _____ in college _____ , _____ I became interested _____ in biology.

4. I'll send you _____ some postcards _____ , _____ when I get to Paris.

5. As the handsome man entered the room _____ , _____ all eyes _____ followed his every move.

6. Oh _____ , _____ you really look wonderful _____ in that dress.

7. Jim _____ , _____ would you help _____ me get the picnic basket _____ , _____ cooler _____ , _____ and blankets _____ from the attic?

8. The boys _____ , _____ as usual _____ , _____ came in from the yard _____ to wash up.

9. Someone asked him _____ "Are you feeling all right _____ , _____ Mr. Dunn?"

10. Our house is at 2890 Miller _____ , _____ Street _____ , _____ Streeterville _____ , _____ Iowa.

Colons

One use of the colon was introduced earlier in the discussion of capitalization—if two or more sentences related to the same topic follow a colon, each sentence should be capitalized. But if there is only one sentence or just a series not contained in a complete sentence, there is no capitalization.

One of the most common uses for the colon is to separate hours from minutes when times are written as numerals.

It's exactly 10:55 a.m.

The last bus leaves the depot at 7:30 p.m.

Unlike an informal or personal letter, which uses a comma after the greeting and closing, a business letter uses a colon after the greeting but still uses a comma after the closing. For example:

Dear Professor Hansen:

Dear Sir:

Sincerely,

Respectfully,

A colon is used between the chapter and verse numbers in biblical references such as the following:

You'll find that in Genesis 1:4.

Semicolon

A semicolon is often used to separate items in a series, especially when commas are used in those items for other purposes. For example:

In the last ten years we lived in Chicago, Illinois; Trenton, New Jersey; and Miami, Florida.

We visited Tom, my husband's former brother-in-law; Louise, his elderly aunt; and Martin Jones, who was a neighbor when his family lived in Montana.

A semicolon can also be used to join two independent clauses.

> My sister was dancing onstage; I was recording her performance on my cell phone.
>
> Jake hated math; he struggled with his homework every evening.

Quotation marks

Statements in direct discourse are placed between quotation marks. For example:

> The teacher said, "You've made a lot of progress, Eric."
>
> "Don't be afraid to use all your strength," Coach Brown told the team.
>
> "Ow! That hurts!" the little boy bellowed.

If the punctuation mark at the end of a sentence that contains a quotation is used for the entire sentence, the punctuation mark is placed after the final quotation. If the punctuation mark is part of the quotation, it appears inside the final quotation mark.

> Why did the officer say, "There's no real danger here"?
>
> Billy asked in a sleepy voice, "Do I really have to go to bed now?"

In the first example, the **question** is *Why did the officer say that?* (*that* meaning the quotation "There's no real danger here.") The officer's statement, however, is a **declarative sentence**, not a question. Therefore, the question mark follows the quotation marks. In the second example, the quotation is Billy's actual question. Therefore, the quotation marks follow the question mark.

Quotation marks are also used to indicate the title of a poem, article, song, or other short works. For example:

> My favorite poem by Longfellow is "Evangeline."
>
> Our daughter gets a little nostalgic when she hears "White Christmas."

Single quotation marks are used inside another quotation. Follow the regular rules for double quotation marks when including a quote surrounded by single quotation marks.

> Laura asked, "Have you read his article, 'The Road to the White House'?"
>
> "My favorite song is 'Amazing Grace'," the old woman whispered.

Quotation marks can be used to emphasize a word or symbol to show that it is of specific interest and not just another word in the sentence.

> People say "advertisement" in two different ways.

Apostrophe

One of the primary functions of the apostrophe is to indicate a possessive in writing and to emphasize that the -**s** ending is not a plural. Singular possessives are formed by an apostrophe plus -**s**. If the word ends in -**s**, an apostrophe can be used alone, but an apostrophe plus -**s** is also acceptable

> Jane's new hairstyle has the other girls talking.
>
> Have you seen Mr. Moss' new car?
>
> Have you seen Mr. Moss's new car?

When forming the possessive of a plural noun, place the apostrophe after the last -**s**.

> The boys' father had to come to school again.
>
> He accidentally walked in on the bosses' weekly meeting.

If the plural is irregular, follow the rules for singular nouns.

> He overheard the women's conversation and became embarrassed.
>
> Your children's behavior has improved a great deal.

When the possessive is made up of more than one noun, its meaning has two forms. One shows that two people own the same object, and one shows that two people own two different but similar objects. With the former, use an apostrophe and -**s** only after the second person mentioned. With the latter, use an apostrophe with both people. For example:

> Did you see John and Mary's new cars? *(They have two new cars. The cars belong to both of them.)*
>
> Did you see John's and Mary's new cars? *(They each have a new car.)*

Apostrophes are also used to indicate that a letter or number has been omitted. This is particularly true of contractions.

Contractions

I am	=	I'm feeling rather ill.
you are	=	You're in the army now.
he is	=	He's my best friend.
cannot	=	I can't understand you.
they will	=	They'll be home by tomorrow.
it was	=	'Twas the night before Christmas.

When a portion of a number is omitted, an apostrophe can stand where the omitted number had been. For example:

Numbers

1958	=	My grandfather was born in '58.
1990s	=	I thought the '90s were a great time.

Some English speakers confuse the position of the apostrophe with numbers and use one when the number is just a plural and nothing has been omitted.

> The 1920s were wild. *(not 1920's)*
>
> An interesting period was the Gay '90s. *(not 90's)*
>
> The 2000s had a lot of economic problems. *(not 2000's)*

But numbers can occur in the possessive, and they use an apostrophe to indicate that possessive.

> The 1960s' riots were often a response to the Vietnam War. *(riots of the 1960s)*
>
> I love the '80's music. *(music of the '80s)*

Hyphen

The hyphen is sometimes taken for granted as a simple form of punctuation. But it has its difficulties. One of them is its use in syllabification. When long words *wrap around* at the end of a line, one or more syllables have to appear on the next line. Syllabifying correctly is important.

Separate syllables tend to begin with a consonant. Some examples:

advertisement	=	ad-ver-tise-ment
constitution	=	con-sti-tu-tion
notification	=	no-ti-fi-ca-tion

But in some cases, a syllable will begin with a vowel or be a vowel that stands alone as a syllable.

deity	=	de-i-ty
faculty	=	fac-ul-ty
mariner	=	mar-i-ner

When in doubt about syllabification, refer to a dictionary.

Hyphens are also used to make compound words, that is, words that are combined to make a new word or to alter the meaning of a word. For example:

father-in-law

six-pack

mass-produced

Words combined by a hyphen tend to be nouns or adjectives. Many come from a verb phrase. For example:

These goods are produced on a massive scale.	=	These are **mass-produced** goods.
We tried **finding** the **facts**.	=	He's on a **fact-finding** mission.
I **warmed up** with a lap around the track.	=	You need a twenty-minute **warm-up**.
Do you **know how** to do that?	=	I just don't have the **know-how**.
Her stories about India really **opened my eyes**.	=	Her stories were real **eye-openers**.

Other compound words are derived from other parts of speech as well as verbs.

We're here for the **long term**.	=	This is a **long-term** agreement.
We'll finish the project at the **end** of the **year**.	=	It will be our **year-end** project.
She wants to **be well** again.	=	I worry about her **well-being**.
I **wore out** three pairs of shoes.	=	These shoes are completely **worn-out**.
The athlete is quite **able** and has a good **body**.	=	He is an **able-bodied** wrestler.

When numbers from 21 to 99 or fractions are written out, they become compound words combined by a hyphen.

I can't wait to turn **twenty-one**.

There are **sixty-seven** applicants for the same job.

She used **three-fourths** of the butter for the cookies.

I bought **seven-tenths** of a yard of canvas.

In the blank provided, write an original sentence with the phrase in bold used as an adjective. For example:

I **know how** to do that.

Does he have the know-how to handle the job?

1. This **class** of people is **working** for itself.

   _____

2. That judge has a **narrow mind**.

   _____

3. They say that John has a **strong will**.

   _____

4. He came back from the hunt with his **hands empty**.

   _____

5. This movie is **packed** with **action**.

   _____

6. The nanny **spoke** very **softly**.

   _____

7. They went on the journey for **one time** only.

   _____

8. Men in this profession wear **white collars**.

   _____

9. They took her picture very **close up**.

   _____

10. These problems **consume** a lot of our **time**.

    _____

11. These telephone wires run a **long distance**.

    _____

12. The little boy is **five years old**.

    _____

13. That mountain is **far off** in the distance.

    _____

14. His daughter has **blond hair**.

_____

15. We have our inventory at the **end** of the **year**.

_____

Rewrite each sentence, capitalizing nouns that need a capital letter and adding the punctuation that has been omitted. For example:

when he was in detroit mr jones bought a new buick

When he was in Detroit, Mr. Jones bought a new Buick.

1. their conversation was always one sided but tom didn't complain because he loved her dearly

_____

2. ive always wanted a long term relationship but im worried because I think you like me because im well to do

_____

3. shell get you a printout of the article and you can work on it in my office

_____

4. dont you wonder why ms brown said (quote) i cant believe theyre firing me

_____

5. get your hands off me she shouted at her brother in law

_____

6. the twins were born on june 5 1998 and our six year old was born just two years later on the same date.

_____

7. hes been taking introduction to computer science at the university of chicago since last september

_____

8. in most of asia youll discover that the peoples diet consists mainly of rice beans and fish

_____

9. professor simpson was more than a teacher he was also marvelous speaker he published several books he was even a great ballroom dancer

_____

10. oh no well have to leave for the station by 630 am if we want to catch the seven oclock train to boston

_____

Homophones

Homophones are words that have nothing more in common than that *they sound the same*. Because English speakers have been reluctant to clean up their spelling system, they are chained to a dictionary for life if they wish to spell correctly. Spelling is based more on tradition than on the sound of a word. Homophones are part of this spelling dilemma.

For example, the words **to**, **too**, and **two** have completely different meanings and uses but are pronounced the same way. This was not always true. The number **two**, for instance, was at one time pronounced more like it is spelled. In fact, this ancient Anglo-Saxon word has a long-lost sister in modern German in the form of **zwo** (a variant of **zwei**). **Two**'s pronunciation once resembled that of **zwo**. And the German word **zwo** means **two**.

But it is not the pronunciation of words that makes homophones a problem for both native and non-native English speakers. It is spelling. The reader of this book needs to compile a list of homophones and understand how they are spelled in order to use them correctly. This chapter offers practice with a wide variety of homophones to help with this objective.

Let's look at some homophones and their meanings.

HOMOPHONE	MEANING	EXAMPLE SENTENCE
aid	assistance, help	Can I be of aid to you, ma'am?
aide	assistant, helper	My aide will show you to my office.
ail	sick	What's ailing you?
ale	beer	Give me a tall, cool ale, please.
air	what one breathes	The air in here is stifling.
heir	one who inherits	The heir to the throne is in France.
bailed	pumped water out	They bailed out the boat, but it finally sank.
baled	bundled hay	We baled hay in the hot sun.
bald	hairless	The bald man is buying a wig.
bawled	cried	He bawled his eyes out over the puppy.
bare	naked	She agreed to pose bare.
bear	ursine animal	A bear smelled what we were cooking on the grill.

(continued)

HOMOPHONE	MEANING	EXAMPLE SENTENCE
capital	principal, wealth; seat of government	You'll need plenty of start-up capital.
capitol	government building	The US Congress is located on Capitol Hill.
carrot	vegetable	I finally learned to eat peas and carrots.
karat	measure of gold	Is that fourteen-carat gold?
cent	penny	The matches cost fifty cents.
scent	smell, aroma	There was a strong scent of perfume in the room.
sent	past tense of *send*	Did you get the letter I sent you?
days	plural of *day*	He spent ten days in jail.
daze	bewilder, stun	I was dazed by the bright light.
dear	beloved	You are so dear to me.
deer	ruminant mammal	Several deer are grazing in that field.
dew	condensation	There was dew on the petals of the flowers.
do	perform	Do your homework on the computer.
due	owed	That bill was due on the first of the month.

EXERCISE 3·1

Choose the word that is the correct completion of each sentence.

1. Be a dear/deer and close the window for me.

2. That is a capital/capitol idea.

3. There was an unusual cent/scent/sent in the air.

4. He was hit by the ball and left in a days/daze.

5. How many karats/carrots did you use in the stew?

6. This is a rather refreshing ail/ale.

7. Martha was the only air/heir to her father's fortune.

8. The final payment is dew/do/due on March 1.

9. The bald/bawled gentleman ordered a toupee.

10. An immature dear/deer is called a fawn.

Write original sentences using the following words correctly.

1. aide _____

2. ail _____

3. do _____

4. bear _____

5. capital _____

6. due _____

7. sent _____

8. bare _____

9. too _____

10. days _____

11. dew _____

12. aid _____

13. dear _____

14. daze _____

15. karat _____

16. bald _____

17. scent _____

18. carrot _____

19. cent _____

20. bawled _____

Homophones have one characteristic that is unique: they can be any part of speech—the possessive form of a noun, a conjugated form of a verb, or even a contraction. For example:

HOMOPHONE	MEANING	EXAMPLE SENTENCE
you'll (contraction)	you will	You'll find clean towels in the drawer.
yule (noun)	Christmas time	Yule is a happy season.
lead (noun)	a heavy metal	Lead is no longer used for pipes.
led (verb)	to lead (past tense)	Their commander led the assault.

Words often sound alike because of their regional pronunciations. In North America, it is common to pronoun the letter **T** like a **D** when it is in the middle of a word. For example:

wader	=	a person who wades or walks through water
waiter	=	a person who works as a server in a restaurant
bedding	=	blankets and linens for a bed
betting	=	placing a bet, gambling

Not all people pronounce the letter **T** in this manner, but because so many do, homophones such as these are included in this chapter.

Let's look at more examples of homophones.

HOMOPHONE	MEANING	EXAMPLE SENTENCE
budding	blossoming	He was a budding rock star.
butting	hitting with head or horns	You're butting your head against the wall.
die	perish, succumb	Eventually, everyone must die.
dye	color, tint	Why do you want to dye your hair?
discussed	talked over	We discussed this problem yesterday.
disgust	sicken	Your remarks really disgust me.
doe	female deer	The fawn is looking for the doe.
dough	moistened flour	Tom is making the bread dough.
earn	deserve, work for	You will earn your degree this year.
urn	large vase	The shrub is growing in a large urn.
ewe	female sheep	The large ewe over there is pregnant.
yew	evergreen tree	We have several yews in our yard.
you	second person pronoun	Do I know you?
fair	just	It's not fair. You always win.
fare	money for transport	How much is the bus fare to Vine Street?

Be aware that there can be more than one meaning for some homophones. For example:

fair   1. just   2. not stormy   3. pretty   4. an exhibition or a carnival

This book gives the most prominent meaning.

HOMOPHONE	MEANING	EXAMPLE SENTENCE
flour	meal for baking	Put some flour and milk in the bowl.
flower	a bloom	What pretty flowers!
gait	stride	I can tell by her gait that she feels better.
gate	door in a fence	Please don't let the gate slam.

HOMOPHONE	MEANING	EXAMPLE SENTENCE
gnu	South African antelope	There is a large, male gnu at the zoo now.
knew	past tense of *know*	I knew you were hiding behind the door.
new	opposite of *old*	Marie bought a new car.
he'll	contraction for *he will*	He'll be back from Afghanistan next week.
heal	restore to health	This medicine will help to heal him.
heel	back part of the foot	I have a blister on my heel.
ladder	device for climbing	Find a ladder and get the kite off the roof.
latter	second of two	Your former answer was correct. The latter is not.
metal	substances like iron	You need a strong roof. Make it out of metal.
meddle	interfere	Why does your father meddle in our business?

EXERCISE 3·3

Complete the missing line of dialogue with any appropriate sentence that includes one of the previously illustrated homophones. For example:

Is your husband coming home soon?

Yes, he'll arrive on the four-o'clock train.

1. A wooden gate will rot in this weather.

_____

2. I put milk and butter in the bowl. Do you need anything else?

_____

3. The two large gnus in that pen look angry.

_____

4. Why is that deer so fat?

_____

5. Here comes Uncle Henry. He thinks I don't earn enough money.

_____

6. _____?

The bus ride from here to the new mall costs $2.

7. _____?

   Yes, I love roses and violets.

8. I heard you got a raise in pay.

   _____

9. Grandmother always gives you a dollar, and she only gives me 50 cents.

   _____

10. How did you change the color of your blouse?

    _____

11. _____?

    I think he walks like that because he's drunk.

12. How can we get the cat out of that tree?

    _____

13. Are you going to buy an old house to fix up?

    _____

14. That pot is too small for that large plant.

    _____

15. Why are you limping?

    _____

16. I didn't know you were acquainted with Jack Swanson.

    _____

17. Is that tree an ordinary pine?

    _____

18. The plumbing in our house consists mostly of plastic pipes.

    _____

19. I keep telling you that we have to save money. We can't spend so much, and you need a job.

    _____

20. _____

    Are you going to make bread with it?

You will be given a list of homophones and their meanings. Write an original sentence with each one. For example:

to / too / two

We will fly to California.

This meat is too tough.

I have only $2 left.

1. naval = referring to the navy / navel = belly button

   _____

   _____

2. none = not one / nun = woman devoted to religion

   _____

   _____

3. oar = paddle for moving a boat / or = conjunction meaning *either* / ore = raw mineral

   _____

   _____

   _____

4. peddle = sell a small amount of goods / petal = part of a flower / pedal = lever operated by the foot

   _____

   _____

   _____

5. pudding = flavored dessert / putting = present participle of *put*

   _____

   _____

6. quarts = plural of *quart*, quarter of a gallon / quartz = crystallized silicon

   _____

   _____

7. raise = lift up, elevate / rays = plural of *ray*, beams of light / raze = to tear down, destroy

   _____

   _____

   _____

8. rap = knock / wrap = cover in paper or material

_____

_____

9. rote = mechanical memorization / wrote = past tense of *write*

_____

_____

10. sew = fasten with a needle and thread / so = conjunction meaning *in such a way* / sow = plant seed

_____

_____

_____

11. their = possessive of *they* / there = location in the distance / they're = contraction of *they are*

_____

_____

_____

12. threw = past tense of *throw* / through = preposition meaning *from end to end*

_____

_____

13. wait = rest patiently, await / weight = heaviness

_____

_____

14. wood = product from trees / would = past tense of *will*

_____

_____

15. your = possessive of *you* / you're = contraction of *you are*

_____

_____

_____

Refer to Appendix A for a detailed list of English homophones.

Verb oddities

·4·

English has very few irregular verbs in the present tense. In most cases, those irregularities are hardly complex.

Be

The high-frequency verb **to be** is the most complicated of these verbs, yet it is not a great challenge. Its present tense conjugation is as follows:

	SINGULAR	PLURAL
First person	I am	We are
Second person	You are	You are
Third person	He is	They are
	She is	
	It is	

When this verb occurs in a contraction, whether in a positive or a negative statement, the verb is made into a contraction with the subject. However, a second contraction can be formed with the negative adverb **not**. For example:

	POSITIVE	NEGATIVE
I'm	I'm not	—
You're	You're not	You aren't
He's	He's not	He isn't
She's	She's not	She isn't
It's	It's not	It isn't
We're	We're not	We aren't
They're	They're not	They aren't

Note that the phrase **I am** does not form a contraction with **not**.

When these contractions are used in a question, the verb in a positive question does not form a contraction. A contraction only occurs in the negative, and the pronoun **I** uses a new verb—**are**. In a negative question, the adverb **not** is contracted with the verb.

POSITIVE	NEGATIVE
Am I?	Am I not? / Aren't I?
Are you?	Are you not? / Aren't you?
Is he?	Is he not? / Isn't he?
Is she?	Is she not? / Isn't she?
Is it?	Is it not? / Isn't it?
Are we?	Are we not? / Aren't we?
Are they?	Are they not? / Aren't they?

Singular nouns use the same verb and contraction forms as do third person singular pronouns. Plural nouns use the same verb and contraction forms as does the third person plural pronoun. For example:

The boy is	The boys are
The boy's	The boys're
The boy's not	The boys're not
The boy isn't	The boys aren't

Although you will often hear a contraction like **the boys're** in spoken language, it looks awkward in writing and is avoided.

Schoolchildren are discouraged from using the contraction **ain't**. It is considered poor grammar but is found today in a variety of regional dialects in the entire English-speaking world. It is the original negated contraction of **I am not**: **I ain't**. Although originally a contraction used with the pronoun **I**, today **ain't** is used with most any subject.

He ain't feeling well today.
Ain't it hot in here?
We ain't going to work tomorrow.

This description is not meant to encourage the use of **ain't**; rather, it is an explanation for this verb form's existence and widespread usage.

EXERCISE
4·1

Rewrite each sentence, changing the subject and verb to a contraction. Then rewrite the same sentence using the two forms of negative contractions and as a negative question with a contraction. For example:

She is pretty.

She's pretty.

She's not pretty.

She isn't pretty.

Isn't she pretty?

1. That girl is my sister.

_____

_____

_____

_____

2. We are tired.

_____

_____

_____

_____

3. You are a good friend.

_____

_____

_____

_____

4. They are at home.

_____

_____

_____

_____

5. He is strong.

_____

_____

_____

_____

Have

The verb **have** and a few verbs that end in a vowel need some explanation. In the present tense, **have** has a slight irregularity in the third person singular: **have** becomes **has**.

He has brown eyes.
She has a class at 1 p.m.
It has become quite cold.

This verb forms its contractions and negative forms in the same way as **be**. For example:

You have	She has	I have
You've	She's	I've
You've not	She's not	I've not
You haven't	She hasn't	I haven't
Have you?	Has she?	Have I?
Haven't you?	Hasn't she?	Haven't I?

Note that **I** does not require any special attention with the verb **have**.

Verbs ending in a vowel

The verbs **do**, **go**, and **ski** end in a vowel. In the third person singular, **do** and **go** do not just add an **-s** to the verb; they add **-es**. Because **ski** is a foreign word, it does not follow the same pattern as **do** and **go**; its third person singular conjugation just adds **-s**. Let's look at how these three verbs form their contractions and negative forms.

He does.	She goes.	Tom skis.
He does not.	She does not go.	Tom does not ski.
He doesn't.	She doesn't go.	Tom doesn't ski.
Does he?	Does she go?	Does Tom ski?
Doesn't he?	Doesn't she go?	Doesn't Tom ski?

There are two uses of **do**: one is as an auxiliary for negation or a question, and the other is as the transitive verb that means to **carry out**, **perform**, or **execute**. First, let's look at this verb's function as an auxiliary for another verb; in this case, **speak**.

He speaks French.
Negation: He **does** not speak French.
Contraction: He **doesn't** speak French.
Question: **Does** he speak French?
Negation: **Doesn't** he speak French?

Now compare that usage with **do** when it means to **carry out**, **perform**, or **execute**.

She does her homework.	**We do yoga at home.**
Negation: She **does** not **do** her homework.	We **do** not **do** yoga at home.
Contraction: She **doesn't do** her homework.	We **don't do** yoga at home.
Question: **Does** she **do** her homework?	**Do** we **do** yoga at home?
Negation: **Doesn't** she **do** her homework?	**Don't** we **do** yoga at home?

In each of the preceding sentences, the auxiliary **do** accompanies the verb **do** (**carry out**, **perform**, **execute**) just as it does with other verbs such as **speak**.

Do does not act as the auxiliary for **be**. However, it can be the auxiliary for **have** when **have** is a transitive verb and not the perfect tense auxiliary. For example:

BE	AUXILIARY *HAVE*	TRANSITIVE VERB *HAVE*
He is here.	He has seen it.	He has a book.
He isn't here.	He hasn't seen it.	He doesn't have a book.
Is he here?	Has he seen it?	Does he have a book?
Isn't he here?	Hasn't he seen it?	Doesn't he have a book?

Although it sounds very formal or old-fashioned, you will sometimes hear or read **He hasn't a book, Has he a book?** or **Hasn't he a book?**

EXERCISE
4·2

Rewrite each sentence in the negative, in the negative with a contraction, as a question, and as a negative question. For example:

Mary likes Jim.

Mary does not like Jim.

Mary doesn't like Jim.

Does Mary like Jim?

Doesn't Mary like Jim?

1. They spend the summer in Canada.

_____

_____

_____

_____

2. That man has her wallet.

_____

_____

_____

_____

3. She does me a favor.

_____

_____

_____

_____

4. They buy a new SUV.

_____

_____

_____

_____

5. Jessica goes to college.

_____

_____

_____

_____

6. We ski every winter.

_____

_____

_____

_____

In the past tense, many verbs have irregular forms. Regular verbs are easy to form in the past tense, because most simply add the suffix -**ed**. For example:

	LOOK	CARRY
I	looked	carried
you	looked	carried
he, she, it	looked	carried
we	looked	carried
you	looked	carried
they	looked	carried

Only two verbs have an irregular past tense form that is radically different from their infinitive or present tense conjugation. These verbs—**be** and **go**—are hardly recognizable when used in the past tense.

	BE	GO
I	was	went
you	were	went
he, she, it	was	went
we	were	went
you	were	went
they	were	went

Other irregular past tense verbs, however, usually give a small clue in the form of the first letter or two that they are related to a certain infinitive and present tense conjugation. For example:

INFINITIVE	IRREGULAR PAST TENSE
to come	came
to do	did
to drive	drove
to find	found
to have	had
to keep	kept
to make	made
to see	saw
to sleep	slept
to speak	spoke
to stand	stood
to write	wrote

A few verbs in the past tense are identical to their infinitive in form. They are as follows:

INFINITIVE	IRREGULAR PAST TENSE
to beat	beat
to bet	bet
to burst	burst
to cast	cast
to cost	cost
to cut	cut
to hit	hit
to hurt	hurt
to let	let
to put	put
to set	set
to shed	shed
to shut	shut
to slit	slit
to spit	spit (spat)
to thrust	thrust
to wet	wet

A small group of ancient Anglo-Saxon irregular verbs have retained their traditional spelling but are not pronounced in a way that resembles that spelling. Their infinitives and past tense forms are as follows:

INFINITIVE	IRREGULAR PAST TENSE
to teach	taught
to catch	caught

(continued)

INFINITIVE	IRREGULAR PAST TENSE
to think	thought
to bring	brought
to seek	sought
to buy	bought
to fight	fought
to work	wrought (worked)

In some cases, verbs have two forms in the past tense. This occurs when a verb is undergoing a change from having an irregular past tense to having a regular past tense form. Here are a few examples:

INFINITIVE	PAST TENSE
to abide	abided, abode
to bid	bade, bid
to dive	dived, dove
to dream	dreamt, dreamed
to hang	hanged, hung
to kneel	knelt, kneeled
to light	lit, lighted
to mow	mowed, mown
to plead	pleaded, pled
to shine	shined, shone
to sink	sank, sunk
to slay	slayed, slew
to speed	speeded, sped

When these verbs are conjugated in the perfect tenses, the past participle tends to follow the pattern of the past tense; that is, there are sometimes two forms for the participle. For example:

He has **slayed** the dragon.   He has **slain** the dragon.

The thief has **pleaded** guilty.   The thief has **pled** guilty.

The servants have **lit** the candles.   The servants have **lighted** the candles.

There is no such difficulty with irregularities in the future tense, since an infinitive follows the auxiliary **shall** or **will**: **He will slay the dragon. We shall light the candles.**

The auxiliary **shall** is used primarily with the first person (**I** and **we**), although many English speakers use **will** with these pronouns. But in a question, **shall** must be used appropriately.

I **shall** help him with the work. I **will** help him with the work.

Shall I help him with the work?

We **shall** study together. We **will** study together.

Shall we study together?

Rewrite each present tense sentence in the missing tenses. Write the future tense sentence as a question. For example:

He speaks Italian.

PAST *He spoke Italian.*

PRESENT PERFECT *He has spoken Italian.*

FUTURE *He will speak Italian.*

QUESTION *Will he speak Italian?*

1. She brings home a friend.

    PAST _____

    PRESENT PERFECT _____

    FUTURE _____

    QUESTION _____

2. The boys eat all the cake.

    PAST _____

    PRESENT PERFECT _____

    FUTURE _____

    QUESTION _____

3. I cut some bread for sandwiches.

    PAST _____

    PRESENT PERFECT _____

    FUTURE _____

    QUESTION _____

4. You aren't a good musician.

    PAST _____

    PRESENT PERFECT _____

    FUTURE _____

    QUESTION _____

5. The women sew a quilt.

    PAST _____

    PRESENT PERFECT _____

    FUTURE _____

    QUESTION _____

6. Jim doesn't have enough change.

PAST _____

PRESENT PERFECT _____

FUTURE _____

QUESTION _____

7. That rude question cost him his job.

PAST _____

PRESENT PERFECT _____

FUTURE _____

QUESTION _____

8. Mark and Joe don't have enough time.

PAST _____

PRESENT PERFECT _____

FUTURE _____

QUESTION _____

9. We meet at four o'clock.

PAST _____

PRESENT PERFECT _____

FUTURE _____

QUESTION _____

10. Laura speeds down the street.

PAST _____

PRESENT PERFECT _____

FUTURE _____

QUESTION _____

11. I let you try it on your own.

PAST _____

PRESENT PERFECT _____

FUTURE _____

QUESTION _____

12. Jim goes to night school.

PAST _____

PRESENT PERFECT _____

FUTURE _____

QUESTION _____

13. Tim sees a great movie.

PAST _____

PRESENT PERFECT _____

FUTURE _____

QUESTION _____

14. The girls do a project together.

PAST _____

PRESENT PERFECT _____

FUTURE _____

QUESTION _____

15. I am your mentor.

PAST _____

PRESENT PERFECT _____

FUTURE _____

QUESTION _____

Present participles

A verb used in a progressive tense indicates an *ongoing or incomplete action*. In sentences with this verb form, the verb **to be** is conjugated. The accompanying verb is formed as a present participle. This means that the *oddities* of certain verbs do not occur. For example:

COMPLETE ACTION	PROGRESSIVE/INCOMPLETE ACTION
John makes a plan.	John **is making** a plan.
John made a plan.	John **was making** a plan.
John has made a plan.	John **has been making** a plan.
John will make a plan.	John **will be making** a plan.

The verb **to be** can only be used in the present and past progressive tenses: **he is being, he was being**. Using them in a perfect tense or future tense sounds awkward and is therefore to be avoided.

EXERCISE
4·4

Rewrite each present tense sentence in the missing tenses.

1. She is cutting out interesting articles.

   PAST _____

   PRESENT PERFECT _____

   FUTURE _____

2. I am having terrible headaches.

   PAST _____

   PRESENT PERFECT _____

   FUTURE _____

3. James is learning to play the flute.

   PAST _____

   PRESENT PERFECT _____

   FUTURE _____

4. Mr. Gardner is teaching that class.

   PAST _____

   PRESENT PERFECT _____

   FUTURE _____

5. The moon is shining over the lake.

   PAST _____

   PRESENT PERFECT _____

   FUTURE _____

6. Why is that man beating his horse?

   PAST _____

   PRESENT PERFECT _____

   FUTURE _____

7. We are skiing in the Alps.

   PAST _____

   PRESENT PERFECT _____

   FUTURE _____

8. My brothers are going on vacation together.

   PAST _____

   PRESENT PERFECT _____

   FUTURE _____

9. You are being rude.

   PAST _____

   PRESENT PERFECT _____

   FUTURE _____

10. They are buying a house in the suburbs.

   PAST _____

   PRESENT PERFECT _____

   FUTURE _____

Tense usage

·5·

Not all languages use tenses in the same way. English has its own peculiarities, but they are fairly easy to understand. Mastery requires only a little study and practice.

Present tense

The main challenge in each tense is the difference between the verb form that indicates a *complete or habitual action* and the verb form that indicates an *incomplete or ongoing action*. When a verb stands alone and is conjugated in the present tense, the meaning of its action is complete or habitual. For example:

> I speak two languages.
>
> My father works in a bank.
>
> The children play with the dog.
>
> Do you drink tea?

When the progressive form of conjugation (**to be + present participle**) is used in the present tense, the meaning of the verb's action is *ongoing or incomplete*. Compare the following sentences with the previous examples:

> I am speaking with my girlfriend.
>
> My father is working late tonight.
>
> The children are playing with the dog.
>
> Are you drinking tea?

EXERCISE
5·1

Rewrite each sentence using a verb phrase that indicates a complete action in its progressive form. For example:

We go to the zoo.

We are going to the zoo.

1. The children learn about bears.

   _____

2. She writes a letter to her senator.

   _____

3. Does your aunt live in a retirement home?

_____

4. I am very polite to him.

_____

5. The dogs lie in a corner and sleep.

_____

6. Tom has a party.

_____

7. Are you funny?

_____

8. The fraternity brothers build a bonfire.

_____

9. Eric listens to a new rap artist.

_____

10. Do you speak Arabic?

_____

11. Sophia spends a lot of time with her grandmother.

_____

12. They earn money for a vacation.

_____

13. The little boy is naughty.

_____

14. It gets cold again.

_____

15. The roses die.

_____

Past tense

When the complete and incomplete forms of conjugation are used in the past tense, the difference in their meaning and usage becomes clearer. Let's look at some examples.

COMPLETE	INCOMPLETE
He spoke with my uncle.	He was speaking with my uncle.
I read a great article on it.	I was reading a great article on it.
Did you ride the train to work?	Were you riding the train to work?
Bob kissed Ashley.	Bob was kissing Ashley.

A sentence with a progressive tense form can be combined with a subordinate clause that usually indicates some kind of *interruption of the verb's action* and thereby makes it incomplete.

When I arrived, he was speaking with my uncle.

I was reading a great article on Mexico **when my son turned on the TV**.

Were you riding the train to work **when the accident happened?**

When Mr. Smith came into the living room, Bob was kissing Ashley.

It is possible to use the verb that indicates a complete action in the independent clause, but the meaning is completely different. It is not an interruption of the action; instead, it describes *the moment when the action began*. For example:

When I arrived, he **spoke** with my uncle.

The implication here is that he was waiting for me to arrive before he spoke with my uncle. My arrival triggered the start of their conversation, and that action was complete.

Here is another example:

When Mr. Smith came into the living room, Bob **kissed** Ashley.

This sentence implies that Bob was waiting for Mr. Smith to come into the living room before he kissed Ashley. Mr. Smith's appearance in the living room triggered the kiss, and that action was complete.

EXERCISE
5·2

Complete each sentence with any appropriate subordinate clause that begins with **when**. *For example:*

When *Jim saw me*, I was playing with my daughter.

1. When _____, Mary was running to her car.

2. When _____, the boys were singing campfire songs.

3. When _____, we were just pulling into the driveway.

4. When _____, I was just getting out of bed.

5. When _____, the swimmers were diving into the pool.

The subordinate clause is supplied for the following sentences. Complete each one with a sentence that contains a progressive verb conjugation.

6. When I looked into the dining room, _____.

7. _____ when someone turned out the lights.

8. When the fire truck pulled up, _____.

9. _____ when Aunt Vi dropped the roast on the floor.

10. When the teacher turned around, _____.

Sentences such as these consist of (1) a subordinate clause with a verb that indicates a complete action and (2) a sentence that contains a verb indicating an incomplete action. It is possible to place the incomplete action in the subordinate clause and the complete action in the main sentence. Let's look at some examples:

He threw the ball at me when I was washing the car.

When we were dancing, John took a picture of us.

In this structure, it is possible to use subordinating conjunctions other than **when**. For example:

While we were strolling through the park, a cold wind blew over us.

Although Liz was singing beautifully, some of the boys ignored her.

As Tom was approaching the front door, Jim bolted out and knocked him down.

EXERCISE 5·3

Complete each sentence using any appropriate clause and the subordinating conjunction provided.

1. As _____, a flock of birds flew in front of the plane.

2. While _____, he tripped and fell in.

3. Although _____, I couldn't understand a word the man said.

4. When _____, some of the scaffolding collapsed.

5. Because _____, some of the guests had to push past us.

6. Even though _____, he could not become a citizen.

7. Now that _____, you can open a bank account.

8. Since _____, the house should be finished soon.

9. Until _____, he has to be guided by a parent.

10. Unless _____, you will lose your job.

When an auxiliary (**can**, **must**, **have to**, and so on) precedes a verb in a progressive structure, the verb **be** follows the auxiliary and is accompanied by a present participle. Consider these examples:

> You need **to be trying** to find a new job.
> We have **to be working** on these problems.
> You should **be going** to college now.

These same sentences can be stated with a verb that shows a complete action.

> You need **to try** to find a new job.
> We have **to work** on these problems.
> You should **go** to college now.

The difference is simple: when the action of the verb is ongoing or incomplete (**to be trying**, **to be working**, **to be going**), it implies that the action may take a long time to carry out.

Perfect tenses

The present perfect and past perfect tenses are formed in the same way: the auxiliary **have** is accompanied by a past participle. In the present perfect tense, the auxiliary is conjugated in the present tense (**have**, **has**). In the past perfect tense, the auxiliary is conjugated in the past tense (**had**). Both tenses have forms for both a complete action and an incomplete action.

PRESENT PERFECT COMPLETE	PRESENT PERFECT INCOMPLETE
She has stolen the books.	She has been stealing the books.
We have written some checks.	We have been writing some checks.
Bill has worked hard.	Bill has been working hard.

PAST PERFECT COMPLETE	PAST PERFECT INCOMPLETE
I had dated Mary.	I had been dating Mary.
Had you traveled from Egypt?	Had you been traveling from Egypt?
They had fixed the old car.	They had been fixing the old car.

The use of these two tenses is relatively simple. The present perfect tense describes an action that *began in the past and ended in the present*. The past perfect tense describes an action that *began and ended in the past*. For example:

> I have worked here for three years. (*I began my job three years ago. I am still working here today.*)
> I had worked here for three years. (*I began my job ten years ago. I stopped working there seven years ago.*)

A subordinate clause can accompany a sentence in the past perfect tense.

> I had been living in Rome **when I met my future husband**.

> **Until he told me otherwise**, I had believed that he still loved me.

Rewrite each present tense sentence using the tenses indicated.

1. I am learning to speak Japanese.

   PAST _____ I learned to speak Japanese _____

   PRESENT PERFECT _____ have learned to speak Japanese _____

   PAST PERFECT _____ I had learned to speak Japanese _____ had been learning Japanese

2. They sing at the top of their voices.

   PAST _____ They sang at the top of their voices _____

   PRESENT PERFECT _____ they have sung _____

   PAST PERFECT _____

3. Some boys march alongside the soldiers.

   PAST _____

   PRESENT PERFECT _____

   PAST PERFECT _____

4. We are preparing a special dinner.

   PAST _____

   PRESENT PERFECT _____

   PAST PERFECT _____

5. Is Martin going to college?

   PAST _____

   PRESENT PERFECT _____

   PAST PERFECT _____

Future tense

Two forms are used to describe the future: the future tense and the future perfect tense. Both are composed of **shall** or **will** and an infinitive. In the case of the future perfect tense, the infinitive is a phrase using **have** and a past participle.

> **Future**
> He will arrive on time.
> We shall begin the exercise.
> They will escort the ladies home.

Future perfect

He will have arrived on time.

We shall have begun the exercise.

They will have escorted the ladies home.

These conjugations can also have a progressive form, which means that the action is ongoing or incomplete. In the future perfect tense, the structure consists of **shall** or **will** followed by **have been** and a present participle (**will + have been + playing**).

We shall be joining you for dinner.

She will be studying in Paris.

You will have been learning French for a year by then.

They will have been making that quilt for three months by the end of next week.

The future perfect in its progressive form implies that the act has been going on for some time, as in **learning French for a year** and **making that quilt for three months**. It is common to add a phrase that describes when the time for the action of the sentence has been completed, as with **by then** and **by the end of next week**.

Future perfect tense sentences become mired in verb forms. Most often, the simple future replaces them unless a very specific meaning is required. For example:

You will be learning French for a year by then.

They will be making that quilt for three months by the end of next week.

EXERCISE
5·5

Rewrite each present tense sentence using the tenses indicated.

1. Jack describes what he saw.

   FUTURE _____

   FUTURE PERFECT _____

2. No one is rude.

   FUTURE _____

   FUTURE PERFECT _____

3. Are you reading his latest novel?

   FUTURE _____

   FUTURE PERFECT _____

4. The girls look everywhere for the cat.

   FUTURE _____

   FUTURE PERFECT _____

5. Professor Jones is speaking for a long time.

FUTURE _____

FUTURE PERFECT _____

Going

The future tense is often formed with **be going** and an infinitive. This form of the future says that there is *an intention* or *a plan* to do something. For example:

> We **are going** to drive to New Mexico someday.
>
> **Is** John **going** to become a doctor?
>
> What **are** you **going** to do about all your debts?

This structure can also be used in the past tense. The meaning here is that the action was intended or planned at some time in the past.

> Jack **was going** to visit his aunt in Spain.
>
> **Were** you **going** to have the car repaired?

EXERCISE
5·6

Complete each sentence with any appropriate phrase.

1. Is your mother going _____?

2. _____ to spend some time with my parents.

3. Ms. Patel was going _____.

4. _____ to drive to Toronto last week.

5. Are the boys going _____?

Adverbs

The two verb forms (complete/habitual and ongoing/incomplete progressive) can be used with all tenses, but there is another aspect to consider when using these verbs. A sentence that contains a progressive conjugation changes that conjugation to complete/habitual when an adverb indicates that the verb's action occurs more than once. Here are some examples of such adverbs:

> always
> every Monday
> frequently
> never (the opposite of *always*)
> often
> three times a week
> usually

Notice how a sentence changes when one of these adverbs is added.

I am sitting in the living room. I **often** sit in the living room.
We have been waiting for you. We have **always** waited for you.
They will be singing in a choir. They will sing in a choir **every Friday**.

If an adverb is an individual word, it generally appears together with the verb: *He **usually** wears a blue suit.* If the adverb is a phrase, it most often appears at the end of the sentence: *He wears a blue suit **every Thursday**.*

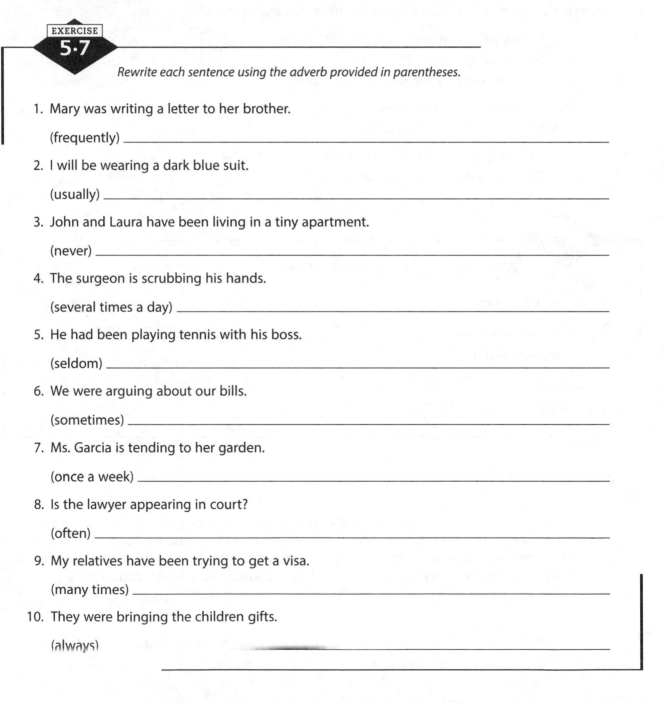

EXERCISE
5·7

Rewrite each sentence using the adverb provided in parentheses.

1. Mary was writing a letter to her brother.

   (frequently) _____

2. I will be wearing a dark blue suit.

   (usually) _____

3. John and Laura have been living in a tiny apartment.

   (never) _____

4. The surgeon is scrubbing his hands.

   (several times a day) _____

5. He had been playing tennis with his boss.

   (seldom) _____

6. We were arguing about our bills.

   (sometimes) _____

7. Ms. Garcia is tending to her garden.

   (once a week) _____

8. Is the lawyer appearing in court?

   (often) _____

9. My relatives have been trying to get a visa.

   (many times) _____

10. They were bringing the children gifts.

   (always) _____
   _____

Passive versus static passive

The active voice is used in a standard statement and is formed with a subject, transitive verb, and direct object. For example:

> I saw the man.
> She has made some cookies.
> The boys will repair that old car.

Passive voice

The passive voice changes the position of the subject, verb, and direct object, but the meaning of the sentence is essentially the same as that in the active voice sentence. The difference is that the subject of the active voice—the doer of the action—is put in a passive position. The passive voice sentence is composed of the direct object used as the subject, the verb as a past participle accompanied by a form of **be**, and the subject now used as the object of the preposition **by**.

> The man was seen by me.
> Some cookies have been made by her.
> That old car will be repaired by the boys.

Some say that the passive voice should be avoided. Despite such a claim, the passive voice is found in speech and written material in great abundance—even in this very sentence. It is a good choice when the speaker or writer wishes to avoid pointing out the subject in an active voice. For instance, this obscures the guilt of a perpetrator of an unpleasant or even illegal act, which cannot be done in an active sentence. Consider the following active voice sentence, which says clearly who the thief is:

> The mayor stole money from the city treasury.

But when that sentence is expressed in the passive voice, the same meaning can be retained or the guilty party omitted, and the basic meaning is altered only slightly.

> Money from the city treasury was stolen by the mayor.
> Money was stolen from the city treasury.

The English passive voice can be described by the following three statements:

1. The direct object in the active voice sentence becomes the subject of the passive voice sentence: **money from the city treasury**.

2. The verb in the active voice sentence becomes a past participle and is accompanied by the verb **be** conjugated in the verb tense used in the active voice sentence: **was stolen**.

3. The subject of the active voice sentence becomes the object of the preposition **by**: **by the mayor**.

This same pattern is used to change other active voice sentences to the passive voice. For example:

ACTIVE	PASSIVE
John will kiss Mary.	Mary will be kissed by John.
That woman has bought a BMW.	A BMW has been bought by that woman.

Rewrite each sentence in the passive voice, retaining the tense of the active voice verb. Then write the passive voice sentence again, omitting the doer of the action or guilty party. For example:

John breaks our lawnmower.

Our lawnmower is broken by John.

Our lawnmower is broken.

1. My sister has sold the puppies.

   _____

   _____

2. The storm badly damaged three houses.

   _____

   _____

3. Ms. Patel will write a book on the subject of art history.

   _____

   _____

4. A terrible fire had destroyed the town hall.

   _____

   _____

5. My brother trains the horses for the rodeo.

   _____

   _____

6. Jim slapped the drunken man across the face.

_____

_____

7. The aircraft carrier transported nearly a hundred planes across the Atlantic.

_____

_____

8. She will write a poem about springtime.

_____

_____

9. The police have captured and arrested the pickpocket.

_____

_____

10. A fallen tree crushed our new car.

_____

_____

Passive voice verb structures can exist in the progressive form just like other verbs and imply that the action is incomplete or ongoing. But the progressive form is only found in the present and past tenses of the passive voice. For example:

Active: The mayor is stealing money from the city treasury.

Passive: Money from the city treasury is being stolen by the mayor.

Active: The mayor was stealing money from the city treasury.

Passive: Money from the city treasury was being stolen by the mayor.

The passive voice verb structure in its progressive form will always be **is being + past participle** or **was being + past participle**.

EXERCISE

6·2

Rewrite the sentences from the previous exercise by changing the passive voice sentences to their progressive form. Take note of how they differ in meaning from the answers in Exercise 6-1.

John is breaking our lawnmower.

Our lawnmower is being broken by John.

Our lawnmower is being broken.

1. My sister was selling the puppies.

_____

_____

2. The storm was damaging three houses.

_____

_____

3. Ms. Patel is writing a book on the subject of art history.

_____

_____

4. A terrible fire is destroying the town hall.

_____

_____

5. My brother is training the horses for the rodeo.

_____

_____

6. Jim was slapping the drunken man across the face.

_____

_____

7. The aircraft carrier was transporting nearly a hundred planes across the Atlantic.

_____

_____

8. She is writing a poem about springtime.

_____

_____

9. The police were capturing and arresting the pickpockets.

_____

_____

10. A fallen tree is crushing our new car.

_____

_____

Other auxiliaries

The passive voice uses auxiliaries to modify the meaning of a sentence in the same way that auxiliaries are used with a single infinitive. For example:

> I **want to** speak with you.
>
> **Were** you **able to** find your wallet?
>
> She **has to** work harder.

The following are some commonly used auxiliaries:

> be able to
> be supposed to
> can
> have to
> may
> might
> must
> need to
> should
> want to

They combine with infinitives to make a verb phrase. When combined with a passive voice structure, the passive voice infinitive is composed of **be + past participle**. It is the auxiliary that changes its conjugation as the tenses change.

> Present: My wife **wants to be invited** to my boss's party.
>
> Past: My wife **wanted to be invited** to my boss's party.
>
> Present perfect: My wife **has wanted to be invited** to my boss's party.
>
> Future: My wife **will want to be invited** to my boss's party.

But consider a sentence with a more complex auxiliary: **A war has been able to be prevented for now**. When passive voice sentences become mired with verbs, the tendency is to simplify. The previous example would be changed to the simple past tense: **A war could be prevented for now**.

EXERCISE

6·3

Write a passive voice sentence or question in the present tense using the auxiliary and transitive verb provided. For example:

can / repair

Can his bicycle be repaired again?

1. must / find

   _____

2. be able to / repair

   _____

3. have to / drive

_____

4. should / question

_____

5. want to / invite

_____

6. be supposed to / reward

_____

7. need to / send

_____

8. may / transfer

_____

9. might / sell

_____

10. can / break

_____

Indirect objects

Transitive verbs are usually accompanied by direct objects. But some of them can also be accompanied by an indirect object—that is, the person *to whom* or *for whom* an action is carried out. For example:

> John gives **his sister** $20. (*To whom does he give $20?* **His sister** *is the indirect object.*)
> She bought **the boy** some candy. (*For whom did she buy candy?* **The boy** *is the indirect object.*)

Indirect objects can be used in passive voice sentences in two different ways: (1) they can become the subject of the sentence; or (2) they can become the object of the preposition **to** or **for**, and the direct object becomes the subject of the sentence. Consider how the following active voice sentence changes: **She bought the boy some candy**.

> **The boy** was bought some candy by her.
> Some candy was bought **for the boy** by her.

Look at another example: **They will send Mr. Carlson birthday cards**.

> **Mr. Carlson** will be sent birthday cards by them.
> Birthday cards will be sent **to Mr. Carlson** by them.

Rewrite each active voice sentence in the passive voice, first with the indirect object as the subject and then with the direct object as the subject.

1. Martin buys the girls some ice cream.

   _____

   _____

2. I am lending my neighbors valuable tools.

   _____

   _____

3. Jack has written her a long letter.

   _____

   _____

4. Ms. Patel will give Mr. Jordan this gift.

   _____

   _____

5. The realtor found me a nice apartment in Brooklyn.

   _____

   _____

6. The farmer feeds the horse oats.

   _____

   _____

7. The mayor is presenting the hero (with) a medal.

   _____

   _____

8. The handsome man brought her some chocolates.

   _____

   _____

9. She was sending him little gifts.

_____

_____

10. Someone will give the homeless man a place to live.

_____

_____

_____

Static passive

The static passive looks like the passive voice, because it consists of a form of **be** plus a past participle. But the static passive describes a *state* or *condition* of the subject of the sentence by using the past participle as an adjective.

How can the two types of passive be differentiated? If the sentence uses a verb in the progressive form, it is in the passive voice.

> The men **are being arrested** for the brawl.
>
> **Was** the bridge **being damaged** by the high winds?

When the passive structure is composed of **be + past participle** alone, some confusion can arise. This is a particular problem when the *culprit* or *doer of the action* of the verb is not named. For example:

> The old church is destroyed by a construction crew. (*passive voice*)
>
> The old church is destroyed. (*passive voice* or *static passive*)

In the second example, it is not clear whether **destroyed** is being used as a past participle or an adjective. It can be either, and it is only the speaker or writer who knows the actual intent of the sentence.

It is possible to run a little test to determine whether a participle is part of the passive voice or being used as an adjective: substitute an adjective (for example, **new**) for the participle. If the substitution makes sense, *it is possible* that the participle is an adjective and that the structure is static passive. If the substitution makes no sense, the participle is part of the passive voice. Look at some examples:

> The girl was being kissed by him.
>
> The girl was being **new** by him. (*Makes no sense. Passive voice.*)

> The beautiful clock was broken.
>
> The beautiful clock was **new**. (*Makes sense. Can be static passive.*)

> The horses have been herded into a pen.
>
> The horses have been **new** into a pen. (*Makes no sense. Passive voice.*)

> My gold watch is repaired.
>
> My gold watch is **new**. (*Makes sense. Can be static passive.*)

Remember that a static passive sentence can be understood as the passive voice if that is the intent of the writer or speaker. Many sentences can be both types of passive. For example:

The goods were stolen.

It is possible that the thief (the doer of action) has been omitted from the sentence (**The goods were stolen by a well-known criminal**). Then the sentence is in the passive voice. It is also possible to substitute an adjective for the participle, and the sentence still makes sense (**The goods were new**). Then it is the static passive.

The point here is that the speaker or writer must choose whether to use the passive voice or an adjective. In many cases, only he or she will know which it is. To ensure the use of the passive voice, include the *doer of the action* in the sentence. Or if it makes sense, use a progressive form of the verb **be**.

EXERCISE
6·5

Write two sentences using the verb provided: one in the progressive passive voice in the present tense and one in the static passive in the present tense. For example:

repair

The window is being repaired by my uncle.

The window is repaired.

1. paint

_____

_____

2. break

_____

_____

3. scratch

_____

_____

4. bend

_____

_____

5. sell

_____

_____

 # Subject-verb agreement

Making a subject agree with its accompanying verb is as simple as determining whether the subject is singular or plural. If the subject is singular, use a singular verb form. If the subject is plural, use a plural verb form. For example:

SINGULAR SUBJECTS	PLURAL SUBJECTS
the man is	the men are
the girl has	the girls have
the teacher sees	the teachers see
the house was	the houses were

It is only in the third person singular that the conjugational ending **-s** is added to most verbs (the girl ha**s**, the teacher see**s**). But this does not occur with certain auxiliaries.

SINGULAR SUBJECTS	PLURAL SUBJECTS
the boy can	the boys can
the girl will	the girls will
the woman must	the women must
the cat may	the cats may

The verb **be** is the only verb that has a complex conjugation in the present tense.

I am	we are
you are	you are
he is	they are
she is	
it is	

And, or, and nor

As simple as subject-verb agreement sounds, situations frequently arise in which the agreement between these two elements does not seem clear. For example, when two subjects are combined by **and**, they become a plural subject and require a plural verb.

My brother and my sister **are** in school.
The man and the woman **speak** quietly.

But when they are combined by **or** or **nor**, a singular verb is required.

My brother or my sister **is** going to help you with the children.
Either the man or the woman **speaks** three languages. I don't know which one.
Neither the policeman nor the driver **knows** how the accident happened.

However, if the second of the two subjects is plural, a plural verb is used.

Neither my brother nor my two sisters **have** the time to help you.
Neither your wallet nor your keys **are** in that drawer.

If the second element is the first person singular pronoun **I**, the verb is conjugated for that pronoun.

Neither Martin nor I **am** interested in this idea.
Either the boys or I **was** responsible for ordering the pizza.

When **either** or **neither** is used as a pronoun and is the subject of the sentence, a singular verb is used.

Both blouses are nice. Either **is** a good choice.
I studied your answers. Neither of them **makes** any sense to me.

Some phrases that accompany a subject give the impression that the subject is plural. But these phrases can be misleading, because they are *parenthetical information* and not part of the subject. For example:

The scientist, **along with** a team of assistants, is planning the next experiment.
Ms. Garcia, **as well as** a contingent of students, was helping in the evacuation.
Her sister, **together with** the other team members, came out onto the field.

EXERCISE
7·1

In the blank provided, write the correct form of the verb in parentheses. For example:

(want) Several men _*want*_ to help search for the missing pups.

1. (be) Neither the others nor I _____ willing to change the date of the dance.

2. (have) Both John Carlson and I _____ entered the race.

3. (do) _____ everyone have to pay a fee?

4. (be) Either the TV or all the books _____ to be moved another time.

5. (appear) The governor, as well as his wife and children, _____ on the stage.

6. (have) Either the microwave or the dishes _____ to be put in storage.

7. (be) There _____ a long column of soldiers marching into town.

8. (want) Neither Jane nor he _____ to be in the play.

9. (play) Mark or his sister _____ the guitar rather well.

10. (write) Both Tom and Laura _____ me letters.

A prepositional phrase often follows pronouns such as **anyone**, **any one**, **anybody**, **each**, **each one**, **everyone**, **every one**, **everybody**, **no one**, **nobody**, **someone**, and **somebody**. These pronouns all require a singular verb, but the object of a prepositional phrase that accompanies one of these pronouns can be plural. This can cause the speaker or writer to use a plural verb erroneously. Here are some example sentences:

> Any one of the boys **is** likely to be nominated.
> Each of the contestants **performs** very well.
> Nobody **wants** to walk that far.
> Somebody **needs** to speak up and tell the truth.

A word of caution with **anyone/any one**, **each/each one**, and **everyone/every one**. The words **anyone**, **each**, and **everyone** are singular pronouns.

> Anyone can understand that.
> Each of you has to climb that rope.
> Everyone needs a kind word now and then.

When **one** stands alone, it is a pronoun, and **any**, **each**, and **every** are modifiers.

> Any one of the men can do this job.
> Each one of the crew members has to learn the safety rules.
> Every one of you is to be rewarded for your service.

EXERCISE
7·2

Complete each sentence with any appropriate phrase in the present tense.

1. Each of the girls _____.

2. Two of the boys are showing progress, but neither _____.

3. Every one of these designs _____.

4. The four pictures are of triangles, but each _____.

5. Not everyone _____.

6. I like both computers, I suppose either _____.

7. I tasted all five cakes. Each one _____.

8. The flute, as well as the clarinet, _____.

9. You all performed well, but not everyone _____.

10. Anybody _____.

Number

The noun **number** is used in a somewhat peculiar way. If it is used with a definite article and is followed by a prepositional phrase introduced by **of**, it is considered a singular noun, and a singular verb is required.

> The number of tickets we needed **was** ten.
> The number of runners in the marathon **comes** to more than three hundred.

If **number** is used with an indefinite article and is followed by a prepositional phrase introduced by **of**, it is considered a plural.

> A number of my students **are** worried about the upcoming exam.
> A number of older workers **have** lost their jobs.

All, *none*, and *some*

The pronouns **all**, **none**, and **some** can be used with a singular or plural verb, depending on the prepositional phrase that accompanies them. If the object of the preposition is singular, a singular verb is used; if it is plural, a plural verb is used. Let's look at some examples:

SINGULAR	PLURAL
All of the fabric **is** ruined.	All of my books **are** ruined.
None of the food **tastes** good.	None of the cookies **taste** good.
Some of the money **was** counterfeit.	Some of the stocks **were** counterfeit.

EXERCISE

7·3

Complete each sentence with any appropriate phrase in the present tense.

1. Some of your friends _____.

2. A number of young athletes _____.

3. None of the coffee _____.

4. _____ all of your time _____?

5. The number of people _____.

6. All of our neighbors _____.

7. Each one of the women _____.

8. Some of the butter _____.

9. _____ anyone _____?

10. A large number of his statements _____.

Time and money

Measurements of time often include a plural noun, but these expressions require a singular form of the verb **be**. For example:

> Eight days **was** a long time to wait for his check to arrive.
>
> Two months **is** the amount of time you have to pay off the loan.

If the amount of time is followed by a verb other than **be**, the verb is plural.

> Sixty years **have** gone by since I was a boy.
>
> Eleven hours **pass** before I finally see the train approaching.

Amounts of money follow a similar pattern: a singular form of **be** is used with plural amounts of money, and a plural form is used with other verbs.

> Ten dollars **is** a lot for that old book.
>
> Two hundred dollars **was** the price of his new bike.
>
> Eight dollars **lay** on the floor. (*eight individual dollar bills*)
>
> Fifty cents **fell** out of his pocket. (*50 cents in individual coins*)

Scissors and *politics*

Several nouns end in **-s** and look like plurals. Most of them are, but some are singular. For example:

Plural nouns

The scissors **are** on the table.

Your pants **look** a bit wrinkled.

Were his trousers cut to the correct length?

Singular nouns

Politics **is** a difficult career to follow.

Mathematics **has** always been my hardest subject.

Measles usually **causes** itching.

The difference between these two groups of words is that the plural nouns are a single object made up of two parts: two blades on the scissors, two legs on pants and trousers. The singular nouns describe one thing but happen to end in **-s**.

Collective nouns

Many nouns are collective nouns. Some examples are as follows:

> army
>
> choir
>
> club

committee

company

family

government

group

jury

team

They describe a group of people as one entity. But it is possible for collective nouns to be considered singular or plural. If the noun is considered a single unit, it uses a singular verb.

> The army **is** looking for recruits.
>
> Our choir **performs** for several local organizations.
>
> **Does** your club meet every Saturday?

But if the members of a collective group are acting individually, a plural verb is used.

> The choir **are** being fitted for new robes. (*The members of the choir try on various robes.*)
>
> The committee **depart** for their homes around 5 p.m. (*The committee members go to different homes.*)
>
> The jury **have** gone into separate rooms to study the evidence. (*The members of the jury have gone to separate rooms.*)

Naturally, many collective nouns can be formed in the plural; in such cases, they always use plural verbs.

> Several governments **choose** to avoid the international meeting.
>
> Two teams **are** struggling to win the state championship.

EXERCISE
7·4

Complete each sentence with any appropriate phrase in the present tense.

1. Five years _____.

2. Our group _____.

3. The sharper scissors _____.

4. This organization _____.

5. _____ your tweezers _____?

6. Four families _____.

7. My pants _____.

8. Civics _____.

9. A new company _____.

10. Time _____.

Verbs and prepositions

Many verbs can be followed by any variety of prepositional phrases. These verbs describe a specific action, and the prepositional phrases describe the locale of the action or how or when it is carried out. Let's look at a simple sentence with the verb **read** and how prepositional phrases enhance the sentence.

> Jim is reading a book.
> Jim is reading a book **about prehistoric times**.
> Jim is reading a book **under a shady tree**.
> Jim is reading a book **during his math class**.
> Jim is reading a book **from my father's library**.

Notice that a different preposition is used in each sentence, and each phrase provides information about some aspect of the sentence: What is the book about? Where is Jim reading? When is he reading? Where did he find the book?

It is clear that prepositional phrases are an important device for enhancing sentences, and most sentences can include a large variety of such phrases. But some verbs and verb phrases can use only a specific preposition to achieve a desired meaning. Let's look at some of these verb-preposition combinations.

VERB PHRASE AND PREPOSITION	MEANING
be concerned about	be worried about something
be concerned with	be seriously troubled with something
be interested in	have a curiosity about something
be involved with	be occupied with something
belong in	be in a place where something is normally located
belong to	have membership in an organization
drink to	toast, make a toast
think about	have someone or something in your thoughts
worry about	be uneasy about

It is important to know which preposition is required with such verbs. People may understand you if you use the wrong preposition. For example:

> I am interested **for** classical music.
> I am interested **of** classical music.

But for clarity and accuracy, it is essential to use the correct preposition with a verb:

I am interested **in** classical music.

To

A group of intransitive verbs that describe motion to a place are frequently followed by the preposition **to** and a phrase that names a destination. For example:

We are driving **to New York**.
I usually walk **to the park**.
They're flying **to Norway**.
The boys run **to the locker room**.
The baby crawled **to the toy chest**.
The young couple strolled **to the shore of the lake**.

Location prepositions

Certain other verbs are paired with prepositions that describe a location rather than a destination. Here are some of the commonly used verbs and prepositions of this type:

I **placed** the books **on** the shelf.
We **put** the glasses **in** the cabinet.
Mary **set** the bowl **on** the table.
He **threw** the ball **between** the trees.
She **drops** her book **next to** the sofa.
Thomas **lays** the letter **near** the bright lamp.

These verbs are transitive and are accompanied by a direct object. The prepositions needed with such verbs introduce a phrase that describes where the direct object is positioned.

The preposition **into** can replace **in** to emphasize that something is moving *to the interior of an object or place.*

I drive the car **into** the garage.
Bring the flowers **into** the dining room.
The nurse inserted the needle **into** the patient's vein.

EXERCISE
8·1

Write an appropriate preposition in the blank provided.

1. I am not interested _____ such a project.

2. Can you put those plates _____ the cupboard for me?

3. The wild horses are galloping _____ the river.

4. Mr. Lopez laid the blanket _____ the bed.

5. We are going to drive all the way _____ Nova Scotia.

6. Please put the floor lamp _____ the sofa and the end table.

7. Are you coming _____ the party tonight?

8. My mother now belongs _____ a political action committee.

9. I am very concerned _____ how you are raising your children.

10. Let's drink _____ Bill. It's his twenty-first birthday.

11. The lights aren't working. Stand _____ the window to read the message.

12. They flew more than a thousand miles _____ Cairo.

13. Marie often thought _____ her family in France.

14. Let's put the bouquet of roses _____ the piano.

15. I carefully slid the sharp knife _____ the drawer.

About, for, and to

Verbs that *provide or seek information* use certain prepositions in the same way. The most common of these prepositions is **about**.

> She **tells about** her vacation.
> They **chat about** the lovely wedding.
> I **write about** it in my column.
> Have you **read about** the new medical discovery?
> The correspondent **reported about** the bank scandal.
> My father never **speaks about** his family.
> I'd like to **ask** you **about** your trip to Florida.
> What do you **know about** Ms. Kelly?
> What did he **say about** his visit to Scotland?

In many instances, **of** can replace **about**, especially with **tell**, **write**, **read**, **speak**, and **know**.

The preposition **for** can also accompany some of these verbs. However, the meaning is different and has nothing to do with providing or seeking information. For example:

> I write **for** a newspaper in Raleigh. (*I am employed as a reporter for a newspaper.*)
> The girl often reads **for** Mr. James. (*For some reason, Mr. James cannot read.*)
> We need to ask **for** your help. (*We are seeking your aid.*)
> What do you have to say **for** yourself? (*How do you explain your behavior?*)

The preposition **to** can also accompany some of these verbs, and again, a different meaning is achieved.

> I often write **to** my relatives in Mexico. (*I correspond with my relatives.*)
> The girl often reads **to** Mr. James. (*She reads a book aloud.*)
> He reports **to** the manager. (*His boss is the manager.*)
> My father is speaking **to** my teacher. (*My father is having a conversation with my teacher.*)
> What did she say **to** him? (*What conversation did she have with him?*)

Write an appropriate verb in the blank provided.

1. I don't _____ anything about this problem.

2. Mr. Henderson said he wants to _____ to my parents.

3. The boys quietly _____ about one of the girls.

4. In June we're going to _____ to Alaska.

5. She never _____ of her ex-husband.

6. Do you always _____ such long letters to your girlfriend?

7. I really don't have anything to _____ about my actions.

8. She _____ about the proposed building in a brief article.

9. My brother _____ a little about what the mayor is planning.

10. I'm afraid I have to _____ for another loan from you.

Let's look at a few more useful verb-preposition combinations.

VERB PHRASE AND PREPOSITION	MEANING
call to	shout to get someone's attention
care for	protect; feel affection for someone
climb up	ascend by climbing
come between	interfere between two people
cry over	regret, weep
fall into	have good fortune with something
laugh at	ridicule with laughter
look into	investigate
settle into	become comfortable in
shout at	yell angrily
stand for	represent; endure or suffer
stare at	glare, look intensively
wait for	await, remain until something happens
watch over	guard, protect

Write an appropriate verb and preposition in the blanks provided. For example:

Next week John *is driving to* Switzerland.

1. The American flag _____ _____ democracy and liberty.

2. I was so embarrassed. They all _____ _____ my clothes and shoes.

3. We understand the problem and will _____ _____ it as soon as possible.

4. Now that the move is over, the couple has _____ _____ their new apartment.

5. Grandma will _____ _____ the children while I take you to the emergency room.

6. I feel so uncomfortable. That man is _____ _____ me.

7. You're late. I _____ an hour _____ you.

8. One of the students came to her desk and _____ her _____ a pencil.

9. Just _____ your coats _____ that chair.

10. A frantic boy was _____ _____ me for help.

11. I like him so much, but I don't think he _____ _____ me at all.

12. If you _____ _____ the ladder, you can reach the cat.

13. There's no reason to _____ _____ your lost wallet. It had nothing in it.

14. I liked to _____ _____ the blind man.

15. Why would he want to _____ _____ those young lovers?

16. He was unemployed for so long. Then one day he _____ _____ a great job.

17. He dropped the cell phone, and his boss began to _____

   _____ him.

18. The women often _____ _____ the news in the neighborhood.

19. I will not _____ _____ this kind of rude behavior again.

20. Jean _____ a political column _____ a New York magazine.

This chapter has provided a limited look at verb-preposition combinations. It is only the first step in mastering such combinations. When learning new verbs, it is essential to know whether specific prepositions are used with them. Incorrect prepositions can change the desired meaning of a sentence or make the sentence impossible to understand.

Subjunctive

9

The subjunctive is a verb form that is used to express *emotion, opinion, possibility, unreality,* or *an action that has not yet taken place*. It has three forms of conjugation that are all used in their own individual ways.

1. The stem of an infinitive becomes the verb with all persons, whether singular or plural. Let's look at this conjugation with three verbs.

INFINITIVE AND STEM		
TO GO / GO	*TO LIKE / LIKE*	*TO BE / BE*
I go	I like	I be
you go	you like	you be
he/she/it go	he/she/it like	he/she/it be
we go	we like	we be
they go	they like	they be

2. The plural past tense form of a verb is used as a subjunctive conjugation.

INFINITIVE AND PAST TENSE		
TO GO / WENT	*TO LIKE / LIKED*	*TO BE / WERE*
I went	I liked	I were
you went	you liked	you were
he/she/it went	he/she/it liked	he/she/it were
we went	we liked	we were
they went	they liked	they were

3. Certain auxiliaries, such as **could, should,** and **would,** become the auxiliary of an infinitive.

COULD, SHOULD, WOULD + INFINITIVE		
TO GO / COULD GO	*TO LIKE / SHOULD LIKE*	*TO BE / WOULD BE*
I could go	I should like	I would be
you could go	you should like	you would be
he/she/it could go	he/she/it should like	he/she/it would be
we could go	we should like	we would be
they could go	they should like	they would be

Present subjunctive

The first subjunctive type is often called the *present subjunctive*, because its conjugation resembles the present tense of the verb. The obvious exception to this is the verb **to be**.

A present subjunctive conjugation is required when certain verbs are used. Some of the most common are **ask**, **command**, **demand**, **desire**, **determine**, **insist**, **order**, **pray**, **prefer**, **recommend**, **request**, **require**, and **suggest**. The use of a subjunctive conjugation is only obvious when using the verb **to be** or with a third person singular subject and a verb in a sentence. First, let's look at **to be** as it is used following one of the verbs in the previous list.

> The judge demanded that he **be** fined for his behavior.
> She recommends we **be** ready by 5 p.m.
> Mark suggested that I **be** careful around those dogs.

These verbs introduce a subordinate clause that requires the conjugated verb to be in the present subjunctive. The use of the conjunction **that** is optional.

Now compare the following pairs of sentences. One in each pair has a third person singular subject, and only with that subject is the present subjunctive conjugation made clear.

> I insist that **you find** a job in the next few days.
> I insist that **she find** a job in the next few days. (*Not she finds.*)

> Laura asks that **the men work** a little faster on the project.
> Laura asks that **the man work** a little faster on the project. (*Not the man works.*)

> Tom prefers **we share** the cost of the rental car.
> Tom prefers **he share** the cost of the rental car. (*Not he shares.*)

EXERCISE
9·1

Rewrite the sentence provided as a subordinate clause with the introductory phrase. For example:

The conductor suggests that _____.

You have your tickets ready.

The conductor suggests that you have your tickets ready.

The angry woman demanded that _____.

1. Someone pays for the accident.

   _____

2. We are better behaved the next time.

   _____

3. The child uses no more naughty words.

   _____

4. I am more helpful in the future.

   _____

5. The pickpocket returns her purse immediately.

_____

I really prefer _____.

6 You speak to me in English or Italian.

_____

7. Your brother is a bit more polite.

_____

8. Ms. Patel learns a different poem by heart.

_____

9. The tourists are ready to depart at noon.

_____

10. It never happens again.

_____

The present subjunctive is also needed after certain standard phrases that introduce a subordinate clause. Some of these phrases are as follows:

It's a bad idea	It is imperative
It's a good idea	It is important
It's best	It is recommended
It's crucial	It is required
It's desirable	It is urgent
It's essential	It is vital

Note that the subject and verb can be stated as a contraction, and the conjunction **that** is optional. Let's look at some example sentences:

It is a very good idea that you be alert when driving at night.

It's urgent he find an emergency room or clinic.

EXERCISE
9·2

Complete each phrase with any appropriate clause that has a third person singular subject.

1. The teacher asked that _____.

2. I insist _____.

3. The old woman desires that _____.

4. The captain commands _____.

5. She finally suggests that _____.

6. The boss recommends that _____.

7. The rules required that _____.

8. No one suggested _____.

9. Headquarters gave the order that _____.

10. Our instructor requested _____.

11. It's essential that _____.

12. It was important _____.

13. It will be required that _____.

14. It's best that _____.

15. It was strongly recommended that _____.

The present subjunctive also appears in a small number of standard phrases that come from the past and are traditional in the English language. Here are some examples:

> Be he beggar or be he king. (*It doesn't matter whether he's rich or poor.*)
> Long live the king! (*We wish the king a long life.*)
> Be that as it may. (*It is possible that that is true.*)
> Come what may. (*It doesn't matter what the future is.*)
> May you know much love. (*I hope you will find love in the future.*)

Past subjunctive

The second type of subjunctive is called the *past subjunctive*, because it is derived from a past tense verb. It is often used as the verb in a sentence that describes *a wish*. Such sentences frequently begin with **if only**. For example:

> If only he spoke a little Spanish.
> If only my wife knew how much I love her.

A perfect tense structure can also be used in these phrases; the past subjunctive verb is the auxiliary **have** followed by a past participle. This structure implies that the wish relates to a time in the past.

> If only she had paid that bill on time.
> If only we had discovered the problem a little earlier.

The verb **wish** can be used to introduce a past subjunctive conjugation.

> I wish my son were back from Afghanistan.
> Jean often wished she had become a professional dancer.
> He wishes he had seen that movie.

The past subjunctive also appears in clauses introduced by **as though** or **as if**. For example:

> That woman talks as though she were so intelligent.
> Why do you act as if you had a solution to this problem?

*Rewrite each sentence following the phrase **if only**. If the sentence is in the past or perfect tense, change the verb to **have** and a past participle. For example:*

She spoke with her boss about it.

If only she had spoken with her boss about it.

1. The weather stays warm.

   _____

2. I did not break that window.

   _____

3. We are better friends now.

   _____

4. She has learned about it from her daughter.

   _____

5. No one heard what I said.

   _____

6. You were not right about it.

   _____

7. I saw that car coming.

   _____

8. The Cubs win the pennant.

   _____

9. Barbara is still my girlfriend.

   _____

10. I have a million dollars.

    _____

    _____

EXERCISE
9.4

Complete each phrase with any appropriate clause.

1. You talk as if _____.

2. The boy behaved as though _____.

3. He glared at me as if _____.

4. Did Jim sing as though _____?

5. They act as if _____.

If

The conjunction **if** has already been shown in expressions that require a past subjunctive conjugation. When **if** is used to introduce a subordinate clause, two kinds of sentences can be formed: one uses a verb in the indicative, and the other uses a verb in the past subjunctive. But the past subjunctive is usually formed from an auxiliary and an infinitive (**could be, should stay, would have**). These sentences set up a *condition* that must be met in order to achieve a *result*. For example:

Condition	Result

If it snows in Denver, it usually snows in Colorado Springs. (*indicative*)

If it snowed in Denver, it would usually snow in Colorado Springs. (*subjunctive*)

If you find some money, you can pay your rent. (*indicative*)

If you found some money, you could pay your rent. (*subjunctive*)

Result	Condition

She is happy if she sleeps until 8 a.m. (*indicative*)

She would be happy if she slept until 8 a.m. (*subjunctive*)

The subordinate clause can begin or end the sentence. For example:

> **If she slept until 8 a.m.,** she would be happy.
>
> She would be happy **if she slept until 8 a.m.**

EXERCISE
9·5

Complete each subjunctive sentence with any appropriate clause. For example:

If you were home, *I would visit you*.

1. If the boys helped me, _____.

2. If you looked in the garage, _____.

3. If I had enough time, _____.

4. If the train got in late, _____.

5. If the teacher understood what I meant, _____.

6. She would go out with me if _____.

7. No one would laugh if _____.

8. The girls would stay longer if _____.

9. The weather would be better if _____.

10. It would be so nice if _____.

Conditional sentences can be written with verbs in a perfect tense. Compare the following pairs of sentences that contrast the simple past subjunctive with a past subjunctive formed like a perfect tense (**have + past participle**).

> If John saw her in the park, he would speak with her.
> If John **had seen** her in the park, he **would have spoken** with her.

> No one would believe him if he suddenly told the truth.
> No one **would have believed** him if he **had** suddenly **told** the truth.

The past subjunctive written with **have** and a past participle implies a condition and result that took place in the past.

Besides **could**, **should**, and **would**, **might** is another auxiliary that is used in the past subjunctive. It usually occurs in the "result" clause and suggests that the outcome is only a possibility. Compare the following pairs of sentences:

> If you asked nicely, I would help you. (*If the condition is met, this will happen.*)
> If you asked nicely, I might help you. (*If the condition is met, this is a possibility.*)

> Jim would stay home if he could watch the game. (*This will happen if the condition is met.*)
> Jim might stay home if he could watch the game. (*This is a possibility if the condition is met.*)

The subjunctive auxiliaries introduced in this chapter all function in the same way but provide different nuances of meaning.

> **Could** suggests an outcome that can occur: **You could become president.**
> **Should** suggests a likely or desirable outcome: **You should become president.**
> **Would** suggests what the outcome will be: **You would become president.**
> **Might** suggests that the outcome is merely a possibility: **You might become president.**

EXERCISE
9·6

Complete each subjunctive sentence with any appropriate clause. For example:

If you had been home, *I would have visited you*.

1. If she had been more careful, _____.

2. I would have spent more time here _____.

3. If _____, I could have taken a nap.

4. If _____, Tom might find a good job.

5. _____ if he had heard his wife's speech.

6. If you could get your wish, _____?

7. She might earn a degree if _____.

8. If _____, nothing would be done about it.

9. _____ if she had known about the party.

10. _____ if they could borrow some money.

11. If Bill hadn't eaten the cake, _____.

12. I could have remained at home if _____.

13. The baby might have slept longer if _____.

14. Her bedroom could look nicer if _____.

15. What would you have said if _____?

Little versus *few*

It may seem strange that an entire chapter of this book is devoted to two simple words: **little** and **few**. But the paragraphs that follow will show that these two simple words can cause a lot of difficulty. Some people find it hard to believe that native English speakers use them so erroneously. Others believe these words to be so similar that they can be used almost interchangeably.

Little

The adjective **little**, which means **small**, does not cause people any problems. It is the opposite of **big** and modifies many nouns with utter simplicity.

> The **little** boy went fishing.
> The puppies are so **little** and cute.

It is the alternative meaning of **little** that marks the start of the usage problems. Its other meaning is the opposite of **much**: *not much, below the usual amount.*

> I have **little** time for nonsense like this.
> The boy has **little** energy left to go hiking.
> The elderly lady needed **little** help to cross the street.

In general, **little** is used with *collective* or *mass nouns*, which are singular: **time, money, energy, water, sugar**, and so on.

Few

The adjective **few** acts in the same way as **little** but modifies plural nouns and is the opposite of **many**: *not many, a small number of.* Here are some examples:

> There were **few** moments when I really enjoyed opera.
> **Few** people in the audience understood his speech.
> He had read **few** books as boring as this one.

Do not confuse **little** with **a little**. The phrase **a little** means something else: *some, a bit of, a small amount*. For example:

> I have **a little** money left. (*some money*)
> Our car needs **a little** push to get out of the mud. (*a bit of a push*)

Also, do not confuse **few** with **a few**. The phrase **a few** means *some, a couple, several*. For example:

> I have **a few** reasons why I don't believe your story. (*a couple of reasons*)
> Take **a few** chocolates home for your children. (*some chocolates*)

EXERCISE 10·1

*In the blank provided, write either **little** or **few** to complete the sentence correctly.*

1. _____ physicians can agree on how to cure this disease.

2. There are so _____ hours in the day to finish my work.

3. He made _____ effort to control the frightened horse.

4. I know _____ men who work harder than Jack.

5. There was _____ milk left in the bottle.

6. _____ arguments ended happily for the husband and wife.

7. There will be _____ agreement on this touchy subject.

8. _____ steel is produced in the Midwest nowadays.

9. There are _____ songs that I would call memorable.

10. She has _____ fear that she will not succeed.

EXERCISE 10·2

*In the blank provided, write either **a little** or **a few** to complete the sentence correctly.*

1. Can I have _____ advice from you?

2. They found _____ old newspapers in the attic.

3. _____ younger children were frightened by the story.

4. _____ care goes a long way.

5. Will she be able to give me _____ help today?

6. Our father always tried to give us _____ encouragement to do well.

7. He spent _____ dollars in just _____ minutes.

8. _____ good luck would be helpful right now.

9. My brother needed _____ long boards for the project.

10. _____ kiss will make _____ men very happy.

EXERCISE
10·3

Write any appropriate sentence using the word or phrase provided.

1. (little) _____

2. (few) _____

3. (a little) _____

4. (a few) _____

5. (little help) _____

6. (few people) _____

7. (a little more time) _____

8. (a few less hours) _____

Comparative

In Chapter 11, the comparative and superlative are described in detail. But the comparative of **little** and **few** must be mentioned here as well, because these forms are often used incorrectly. The basic rules that guide the use of these adjectives accurately are as follows: use **little** with singular, collective nouns; and use **few** with plural nouns.

The comparative of **little** is **less**, and the comparative of **few** is **fewer**. Contrast these words with their antonyms **much** and **many**; like **little** and **few**, they modify singular and plural nouns, respectively.

POSITIVE ADJECTIVE	COMPARATIVE ADJECTIVE	NOUN NUMBER
much	more	singular
little	less	singular
many	more	plural
few	fewer	plural

In sentences, they are used like this:

There is **much** work to be done. There is **more** work to be done.

There is **little** work to be done. There is **less** work to be done.

I have **many** problems. I have **more** problems than you.

I have **few** problems. I have **fewer** problems than you.

In many cases, English speakers overuse **less** and put it together with plural nouns. This occurs in everyday speech, in published advertising, and over the airwaves. But that usage is incorrect. Only singular and collective nouns can be modified by **less**.

> You have **less time** than you think.
>
> She should try to use **less butter** than that.

Some English speakers use **fewer** incorrectly as well, because they have encountered a plural noun and assume that **fewer** is required. However, that is not necessarily the case. The following examples illustrate plural nouns that should be modified by **fewer**:

> I now have **fewer** doubts about the plan than I did before.
>
> **Fewer** people are attending the concert today.

In the following sentences, the plural nouns require the use of **less** rather than **fewer**.

> Is $150 **less** than you'll take for the bike?
>
> Five yards of wool is **less** fabric than I need.

Although $150 and five yards are plural nouns, they are used as a *single unit*—a collective. The issue is not 150 individual dollar bills but a single amount that totals 150. There are not five separate yards of wool but a single length. Notice in the two example sentences that the verb accompanying the two subjects is a singular verb: **is**.

Amounts, weights, and measurements can be used as collectives, and they are therefore modified by **less**. Here are a few more examples:

> Two pounds of sugar **is less** than I need for these cakes.
>
> Twenty years in prison **was less** than his original sentence.

EXERCISE
10·4

*In the blank provided, write either **less** or **fewer** to complete the sentence correctly.*

1. I seem to have _____ hours in the day to do my work.

2. That man shows _____ concern for his children than for his dog.

3. I can't give her _____ money than I give you.

4. We have _____ rabbits in our garden now than we had last year.

5. _____ geese use this pond than the one down the road.

6. Four cups of coffee was _____ than he normally drank at home.

7. I need _____ arguments and more cooperation.

8. Ten miles is far _____ distance than a marathon.

9. Why are _____ women coming to the dance this season?

10. Mr. Bartlett is _____ likable than his wife.

Write any appropriate sentence using the word or phrase provided. **Less** *or* **fewer** *should be used in every sentence.*

1. (less) _____

2. (fewer) _____

3. (six days) _____

4. (cargo) _____

5. (a month) _____

6. (less courage) _____

7. (fewer needs) _____

8. (less) _____

9. (fewer) _____

10. (than) _____

Comparatives and superlatives

The basic form of an adjective or adverb is called the *positive* form. Many adjectives and adverbs in this form are familiar to most people. Here are some examples:

ADJECTIVE	ADVERB
fast	fast
grateful	gratefully
hard	hard
quick	quickly
slow	slowly

To change most adjectives to adverbs, an **-ly** suffix is added. A few words, such as **fast** and **hard**, are exceptions; no change is made to create an adverb.

When an adjective that ends in the suffix **-ful** is changed to an adverb, **-ly** is added just as with other adverbs. Therefore, the adverb will be spelled with a double el: **careful/carefully**, **truthful/truthfully**.

Many adjectives end in **-y**. When they become adverbs, the **-y** is changed to **-i** and then the adverbial suffix is added. For example:

ADJECTIVE	ADVERB
busy	busily
happy	happily

Several adjectives end in **-ly** and look like adverbs. Those few that can be used as adverbs do not change or add a suffix; the adjectival form is used as the adverb.

ADJECTIVE	ADVERB
early	early
friendly	—
homely	—
stately	—

Positive forms of adjectives and adverbs can be used with a common expression composed of **as** and **as**.

She is **as** pretty **as** her mother.

Tom runs **as** fast **as** the best sprinter in our school.

I am not **as** fluent in French **as** Amy.

This kind of statement is not a comparison. Instead, it expresses equality between the two persons or objects mentioned in the sentence. If the sentence is negated, it expresses the lack of equality between the two subjects.

Comparatives

To make real comparisons between people and things, adjectives and adverbs must be expressed in their comparative form. Most adjectives add the suffix **-er**. If the adjective already ends in **-e,** only **–r** is added. If the adjective ends in **-y**, the **-y** changes to **-i** and a suffix is added. The comparative adverb does not add a suffix. Instead, it is preceded by **more**.

POSITIVE	COMPARATIVE ADJECTIVE	COMPARATIVE ADVERB
full	fuller	more fully
quick	quicker	more quickly
sweet	sweeter	more sweetly
tame	tamer	more tamely
busy	busier	more busily

Here are a few exceptions that do not conform to this pattern:

POSITIVE	COMPARATIVE ADJECTIVE	COMPARATIVE ADVERB
early	earlier	earlier
fast	faster	faster
hard	harder	harder

If a positive adjective ends in a vowel followed by a single consonant and consists of one syllable, the same consonant is added to the adjective before the comparative ending is applied. For example:

POSITIVE	COMPARATIVE ADJECTIVE	COMPARATIVE ADVERB
big	bigger	—
flat	flatter	more flatly
thin	thinner	more thinly

EXERCISE
11·1

In the blanks provided, write the comparative adjective and adverb of the positive adjective in parentheses. Not all adjectives will have an adverbial form.

1. (wise) _____ _____

2. (stately) _____ _____

3. (hungry) _____ _____

4. (fat) _____ _____

5. (tall) _____ _____

6. (tense) _____ _____

7. (old) _____ _____

8. (young) _____ _____

9. (bold) _____ _____

10. (angry) _____ _____

11. (gentle) _____ _____

12. (faint) _____ _____

13. (strong) _____ _____

14. (weak) _____ _____

15. (fast) _____ _____

Words of more than one syllable, particularly words of Latin origin, form both the comparative adjective and adverb with **more**.

POSITIVE	COMPARATIVE ADJECTIVE	COMPARATIVE ADVERB
special	more special	more specially
interesting	more interesting	more interestingly
historical	more historical	more historically

The antonym of **more** is **less**. It is possible to use **less** to make a comparison that means the compared person or thing has a smaller amount of the quality expressed by the adjective. For example:

That is **realistic.**

That is **less realistic** than your first suggestion.

He behaves **less realistically.**

In the blanks provided, write the comparative adjective and adverb of the positive adjective in parentheses.

1. (boring) _____ _____

2. (flexible) _____ _____

3. (busy) _____ _____

4. (smart) _____ _____

5. (different) _____ _____

6. (confident) _____ _____

7. (intelligent) _____ _____

8. (accurate) _____ _____

9. (hilarious) _____ _____

10. (sincere) _____ _____

11. (careless) _____ _____

12. (regretful) _____ _____

13. (wise) _____ _____

14. (strange) _____ _____

15. (reluctant) _____ _____

A few positive adjectives form their comparative adjectives and adverbs in an irregular way. For example:

POSITIVE	COMPARATIVE ADJECTIVE	COMPARATIVE ADVERB
bad	worse	worse
far	further	further
good	better	better
little	less	less
many	more	more
much	more	more

The word **far** means *distant* or *advanced in time or degree*; it also means *located in a remote place*. The comparative forms of the latter are regular: **farther** (adjective) and **farther** (adverb).

The adjective **well** can mean *healthy*. When it does, its comparative forms are **better** (adjective) and **better** (adverb.)

A comparative adjective or adverb is used with **than** to draw a comparison between two people or things. The part of the sentence that follows **than** usually has a verb or phrase that is understood and not spoken or written.

He is taller **than** his brother./He is taller than his brother **is**.

She speaks more fluently **than** the others in the class./She speaks more fluently than the others in the class **speak**.

When the comparison is made with a pronoun, the objective form of the pronoun can be used if **than** is used as a preposition. Caution is necessary, because the meaning is different when **than** is used as a conjunction. For example:

USE	COMPARISON	MEANING
Preposition	She likes me more **than him**.	She likes me more than she likes him.
Conjunction	She likes me more **than he**.	She likes me more than he likes me.

Write the necessary form of the adjective in parentheses in the blank provided. For example:

(tall) John is _taller_ than the other boys.

1. (large) My neighbor's garden is very _____.

2. (good) I hope you will earn a _____ grade than last week.

3. (far) We walked _____ than any of the other hikers.

4. (likable) I find that Marie is more _____ than her sister.

5. (bad) His grammar is as _____ as mine.

6. (well) I hope you feel _____ soon.

7. (many) Mr. Jones has _____ books than the school library.

8. (little) We have _____ time to finish this project than we had on the last one.

9. (ridiculous) That hat looks _____ on you than the red one.

10. (bad) Her party was much _____ than Jim's.

Native English speakers often use the comparative adjective form where an adverb is needed. This is done in casual or colloquial speech. For example:

> When he saw her, his heart beat **quicker**.
> I can't keep up. Walk **slower**.
> After a glass of wine, Jim began to act **sillier**.

Superlatives

The superlative form of an adjective or adverb describes a person or thing with the highest quality of the meaning of the adjective or adverb: *no one or nothing is superior.* Forming the superlative of adjectives follows the rules for comparatives only adding **-(e)st** in place of **-er**. To form the superlative of most adverbs, **most** is placed in front of the adverb. Take note that the superlative adjective or adverb can be preceded by **the**.

POSITIVE	SUPERLATIVE ADJECTIVE	SUPERLATIVE ADVERB
slow	(the) slowest	(the) most slowly
quick	(the) quickest	(the) most quickly
happy	(the) happiest	(the) most happily
fast	(the) fastest	(the) fastest

With polysyllabic words, primarily of a Latin origin, **most** is used to form all superlatives.

POSITIVE	SUPERLATIVE ADJECTIVE	SUPERLATIVE ADVERB
independent	(the) most independent	(the) most independently
tasteful	(the) most tasteful	(the) most tastefully
difficult	(the) most difficult	(the) most difficultly

A few positive adjectives form their superlative adjectives and adverbs in an irregular way. For example:

POSITIVE	SUPERLATIVE ADJECTIVE	SUPERLATIVE ADVERB
bad	(the) worst	(the) worse
far	(the) furthest	(the) furthest
good	(the) best	(the) best
little	(the) least	(the) least
many	(the) most	(the) most
much	(the) most	(the) most

The word **the** is sometimes optional when using a superlative as a predicate nominative. The meaning of the sentence is not changed whether it is included or omitted. For example:

> This novel is **the best**./This novel is **best**.
> Is his daughter **the thinnest**?/Is his daughter **thinnest**?

The same rule applies to adverbs.

> Mary runs **the fastest**./Mary runs **fastest**.

But superlative adjectives that modify a noun directly must be accompanied by **the** or some other determiner. For example:

> **The tallest** boy isn't **the best** basketball player.
> **His youngest** children are very polite.
> Give me **your finest** chocolates.

It is possible to use **least** to make a superlative that means the person or thing in question has the smallest amount of the quality expressed by the adjective. For example:

> He is **the least** talented boy in the play.
> His performance was **the least** impressive.

EXERCISE
11·4

Using the adjective provided, write a sentence in the specified form. For example:

(thin/comparative) *My hair is thinner now than a year ago.*

1. (bad/comparative) _____

2. (rapid/superlative adverb) _____

3. (tiny/superlative) _____

4. (rich/superlative) _____

5. (young/positive) _____

6. (new/superlative) _____

7. (fragrant/superlative) _____

8. (delicious/comparative) _____

9. (cozy/comparative with *less*) _____

10. (difficult/superlative with *least*) _____

11. (simple/positive) _____

12. (old/superlative) _____

13. (good/superlative) _____

14. (far/comparative) _____

15. (beautiful/superlative adverb) _____

16. (ugly/comparative) _____

17. (warm/superlative) _____

18. (cold/superlative) _____

19. (wealthy/superlative with *least*) _____

20. (quick/superlative adverb) _____

Pronoun varieties

Personal pronouns

The personal pronouns are described as *first person*, *second person*, and *third person* pronouns. Some are singular in form, and others are plural. For example:

	SINGULAR PRONOUNS	PLURAL PRONOUNS
first person	I	we
second person	you	you
third person	he, she, it	they
	one	

The first person pronouns refer to the speaker or, if plural, speakers: **I feel well today. We are learning English.** The second person pronouns refer to the person or persons to whom one is speaking: **Are *you* new here, madam? Are *you* new here, ladies?**

The third person pronouns play an enormous role in English. Besides **he**, **she**, and **it**, there are numerous others that will be discussed in this chapter. The third person pronouns refer to someone or something that is the topic of conversation without actually naming that person or thing after the first mention. For example:

That's John Brown. **He** is my new neighbor.

Do you know that woman? **She** lives in the apartment next to mine.

Did you lose this wallet? My wife said she found **it** on the sidewalk.

Those boys lied to the teacher. **One** should never lie to anyone.

One is a third person pronoun that is intentionally vague. It does not refer to anyone in particular. It stands for *anyone* or *any person in general*.

One needs to stay alert. (*People in general need to stay alert.*)

One is replaced by the second person **you** in more casual speech, but the meaning is still *anyone* or *any person in general*.

You need to stay alert.

All personal pronouns have more than one form, depending on the pronoun's role in a sentence. Let's look at those forms.

SUBJECTIVE CASE	OBJECTIVE CASE	POSSESSIVE	REFLEXIVE
I	me	my, mine	myself
you (*s.*)	you	your, yours	yourself
he	him	his, his	himself
she	her	her, hers	herself
it	it	its, its	itself
we	us	our, ours	ourselves
you (*pl.*)	you	you, yours	yourselves
they	them	their, theirs	themselves
one	one	one's	oneself

These forms have the same function for all the pronouns. Let's look at some examples with the pronoun **he**:

Subject of sentence	**He** lives on Elm Street.
Direct object	Do you know **him**?
Object of preposition	I had a long talk with **him**.
Indirect object	She gave **him** a large, red apple.
Possessive determiner	This is **his** new car.
Possessive pronoun	**His** is the one parked near the corner.
Reflexive	John cut **himself** on a piece of broken glass.

As shown here, the possessive has two forms. The determiner is used like an adjective and modifies a noun: **his new car**. The possessive pronoun replaces the example noun **car**: **His** is the one parked near the corner.

EXERCISE
12·1

Write sentences using the pronoun in parentheses and the forms specified. For example:

(I)

Subject of sentence: *I bought a blue dress.*

Direct object: *She wanted to photograph me.*

1. (I)

   SUBJECT OF SENTENCE _____

   DIRECT OBJECT _____

   OBJECT OF PREPOSITION _____

2. (you *s.*)

   DIRECT OBJECT _____

   OBJECT OF PREPOSITION _____

   INDIRECT OBJECT _____

3. (she)

OBJECT OF PREPOSITION _____

INDIRECT OBJECT _____

POSSESSIVE DETERMINER _____

4. (we)

INDIRECT OBJECT _____

POSSESSIVE DETERMINER _____

POSSESSIVE PRONOUN _____

5. (they)

POSSESSIVE DETERMINER _____

POSSESSIVE PRONOUN _____

REFLEXIVE _____

EXERCISE
12·2

Write original sentences using the nouns or pronouns provided in parentheses as subjects. Include the corresponding reflexive pronoun in each sentence. For example:

(he) *He injured himself in a fall.*

1. (I) _____

2. (you *s.*) _____

3. (she) _____

4. (it) _____

5. (we) _____

6. (you *pl.*) _____

7. (they) _____

8. (my sister) _____

9. (one) _____

10. (our neighbors) _____

Third person pronouns play an enormous role in English, because they are replacements for nouns. Just imagine how many nouns there are in English. Language loses its awkward sound when a pronoun is used in place of a noun that would otherwise have to be repeated many times. Compare the following two groups of sentences.

> **The train** pulled into the station. **The train** was late again, and **the train** would not be able to make up for the lost time.

> **The train** pulled into the station. **It** was late again, and **it** would not be able to make up for the lost time.

If a noun is singular, it has to be replaced by a singular pronoun, and that pronoun must reflect the gender of the noun: **he** (*masculine*), **she** (*feminine*), and **it** (*neuter*). If a noun is plural, it has to be replaced by the plural pronoun **they**. Naturally, how the noun is used (*subject, object, possessive*) determines which form of the pronoun is used.

EXERCISE
12·3

Replace the underlined noun or noun phrase with the correct pronoun.

1. The men knew they had to work harder.

   _____

2. I came across a large carton of books.

   _____

3. We spoke with Ms. Carlson about that yesterday.

   _____

4. Maria's mother is in the hospital.

   _____

5. Can you understand the lyrics to this song?

   _____

6. Our landlady raised our rent again.

   _____

7. I think I saw your son at soccer practice today.

   _____

8. I bought her car for a pretty good price.

   _____

9. Can you describe the thieves for me?

   _____

10. She borrowed the books from Mr. Kelly.

   _____

Replace each underlined phrase with the correct possessive pronoun.

1. Do you have <u>his notebook</u>?

   _____

2. The boys don't have <u>their tools</u> with them.

   _____

3. <u>Its new nest</u> is hidden behind those bushes.

   _____

4. Have you seen <u>our new SUV</u>?

   _____

5. I think I found <u>your briefcase</u> in the basement.

   _____

6. Is <u>my credit card</u> in that drawer?

   _____

7. I really like <u>her blouse</u> a lot better than <u>my blouse</u>.

   _____

8. Someone took <u>their garden equipment</u> from the shed.

   _____

9. The police said that <u>our version of the accident</u> made more sense.

   _____

10. Did you really lose <u>your keys</u> again?

    _____

Singular or plural verbs

When possessive pronouns are used as the subject of a sentence, the appropriate verb form—singular or plural—also must be used. If the possessive pronoun replaces a singular subject, a singular verb form is used. If it replaces a plural subject, a plural verb form is correct. For example:

> My brother was in the army for two years. (*brother = singular noun*)
> **Mine** was in the army for two years.

> My brothers were in the army for two years. (*brothers = plural noun*)
> **Mine** were in the army for two years.

The verb that accompanies the noun subject and the possessive pronoun subject are singular and plural, respectively. Possessive pronouns can accompany either a singular or a plural verb, depending on the number of the noun they replace.

EXERCISE
12·5

Write two original sentences using the possessive pronoun given in parentheses. Use a singular verb with one and a plural verb with the other. For example:

(mine)

Mine is in my bedroom.

Mine are probably still downstairs.

1. (yours)

_____

_____

2. (his)

_____

_____

3. (hers)

_____

_____

4. (ours)

_____

_____

5. (theirs)

_____

_____

Other pronoun forms

There are other third person pronoun forms as well. Among them are the *indefinite pronouns*. Some of the most common are as follows:

REPLACES A SINGULAR NOUN	REPLACES A PLURAL NOUN	REPLACES SINGULAR OR PLURAL NOUNS
anybody/anyone	both	all
anything	few	any
each	several	most

REPLACES A SINGULAR NOUN	REPLACES A PLURAL NOUN	REPLACES SINGULAR OR PLURAL NOUNS
either		none
everybody/everyone		some
everything		
neither		
nobody/no one		
nothing		
one		
somebody/someone		
something		

Here are some example sentences:

Singular verb

Everybody **knows** not to tease a wild animal.

The two boys play the piano. Neither **has** much talent.

Something **is** wrong with our car.

Plural verb

The two girls sing well. Both **have** lovely voices.

Many tourists visit the castle. Few **understand** how long it took to build.

They are excellent basketball players. Several **come** from abroad.

Singular or plural verb

Your treasure is in that box. All **has** been kept safe for you. (*all of it = singular*)

The books are stored on the third floor. All **need** binding repair. (*all of them = plural*)

There is plenty of cake left. Most **is** for you. (*most of it = singular*)

About 20 teenagers came to our house. Most **are** good friends of mine. (*most of them = plural*)

I found an old manuscript. Some **seems** to be written in French. (*some of it = singular*)

We saw many squirrels in the park. Some **were** quite friendly. (*some of them = plural*)

Demonstrative, interrogative, and reciprocal pronouns are easy to use. The demonstrative pronouns are **this** and **that** to modify singular nouns and **these** and **those** to modify plural nouns.

MODIFIED NOUN	DEMONSTRATIVE PRONOUN
This book is quite old.	This is quite old.
That man is my grandfather.	That is my grandfather.
These shirts are wrinkled.	These are wrinkled.
Those cars were made in Europe.	Those were made in Europe.

The interrogative pronouns *pose questions*. They are **who, whom, whose, what,** and **which.**

Who is that fellow? With **whom** did he speak?

He doesn't have a car. **Whose** is he driving?

What was done about the problem?

The three skirts are very nice. **Which** do you really want?

There are only two forms of reciprocal pronouns: **each other** and **one another**. They can be used interchangeably. For example:

We have known **each other** for many years. We have known **one another** for many years.
They bought **each other** gifts. They bought **one another** gifts.

EXERCISE
12·6

Complete each line with any appropriate phrase using the pronouns provided.

1. Several children were on the playground. Each _____.

2. The two pups slept together. Neither _____.

3. _____ each other _____.

4. Whom _____?

5. That vase is quite valuable, but this _____.

6. There were nine watches in that case. Several _____.

7. There's a lot of pizza left. Most _____.

8. I read the paragraph over and over, but nothing _____.

9. _____ one another _____.

10. The order of steel arrived today, and all _____.

Quantifiers

There are numerous pronouns and phrases called *quantifiers* that describe an amount or quantity of something. Some replace plural nouns, such as **many**, **a few**, **few**, **several**, and **a couple**.

REPLACED PLURAL NOUN	PRONOUN QUANTIFIER
men	**Many** work in the city.
problems	**Few** have ever been solved by a committee.
jokes	**A couple** are really terribly funny.

Other pronoun quantifiers replace collective nouns or nouns that are considered to be a single unit. Some of these quantifiers are **a bit**, **a good deal**, **a little**, **little**, and **much**.

COLLECTIVE NOUN	PRONOUN QUANTIFIER
smoke	**A little** is blowing into their tent.
money	**A good deal** is meant to be yours someday.
cake	Only **a bit** was left on the plate.

Several pronoun quantifiers replace either plural or collective nouns; these quantifiers include **all, a lot, lots, enough, most, none, plenty,** and **some.**

PLURAL OR COLLECTIVE NOUN	PRONOUN QUANTIFIER
trees	**All** have to be chopped down for the highway.
sugar	**All** is needed for the pies.
people	Not **enough** have voted yet.
milk	Is **enough** left for the cats?
tourists	**Some** are from Asia.
soup	**Some** was spilled on the kitchen floor.

EXERCISE
12·7

Complete each sentence using the pronouns provided in any appropriate phrase.

1. Those suits cost $200, but lots _____.

2. There are so many rabbits here. Several _____.

3. The students studied diligently, but few _____.

4. We spent a great deal of time on the project. Much _____.

5. We needed coal as fuel, and finally enough _____.

6. There isn't enough heat. Most _____.

7. I explained my position to the members, but none _____.

8. The stew was for our dinner. Some _____.

9. All the players are angry with their poor performance. Plenty _____.

10. The students in the audience cheer. A few _____.

Determiners and adverbs of degree

Most often *determiners* are described as specific parts of speech, such as **definite articles**, **indefinite articles**, **ordinal numbers**, **possessives**, and so on. These parts of speech can *modify* nouns or pronouns, but they do so in a unique way: determiners give the word they modify quantity, location, and significance.

If the determiner is a definite article, it specifies the modified word as a known entity—the topic of conversation. If the determiner is an indefinite article, it generalizes the modified word. For example:

> **the** toy (a specific toy): The toy on the floor seems to be broken.
>
> **a** toy (toys in general): A toy might be a good gift for little Bobby.
>
> **the** suit (a specific suit): The suit he is wearing looks expensive.
>
> **a** suit (suits in general): A suit made of wool may be too warm for this climate.

Refer to Chapter 1 for more details about the differences between definite and indefinite articles.

Demonstratives

Demonstratives describe *which one* when modifying a noun or suggest the noun's location as near or far. For example:

> **Which one?**
>
> **which:** Which book do you want? They all seem interesting.
>
> **Located near**
>
> **this:** This house belongs to our family doctor.
>
> **these:** These men are employed in the airline industry.
>
> **Located far**
>
> **that:** That woman across the street is Professor Lang.
>
> **those:** Those airplanes in the distance look like bombers.

Articles as determiners specify or generalize, and demonstratives as determiners locate. Usually placed after articles or demonstratives, adjectives describe the *attributes* of a noun. Here are some examples:

> The **funny** clowns made the children laugh.
>
> A **silk** scarf might be a **good** gift for Aunt Helen.
>
> Will they be able to help this **wounded** man?
>
> That **tall** building over there is a **new** hotel.
>
> These **young** men are stronger than those **old** men.

In the blank provided, write an adjective that describes the attributes of the noun. For example:

This _old_ book is quite valuable.

1. The _____ meeting will be on Friday.

2. Those _____ women belong to the same club.

3. Which _____ blouse do you like?

4. I need a _____ blanket.

5. Have you met these _____ students yet?

6. I really want to dance with that _____ girl over there.

7. Do you have a _____ pair of shoes in brown?

8. Yesterday I received this _____ letter in the mail.

9. Those _____ gloves don't belong to me.

10. Which _____ coat is warmer?

Possessives

The possessive determiners are **my, your, his, her, its, our, their, one's,** and **whose**. Their function is simple: they identify ownership. They can be combined with adjectives that describe the attributes of the modified noun. For example:

> My **new** car already has a scratch on it.
> Did your **recent** accident leave you injured?
> Our **finest** wines are kept under lock and key.
> One's **angry** voice is a signal that one is not being rational.
> Whose **ragged** pants and shirt are these?

Ordinal numbers and quantifiers

When an ordinal number modifies a noun, it merely describes a quantity or amount. An accompanying adjective describes the attributes of the noun.

> **One** boy is worried about his future.
> One **lonely** boy is worried about his future.
>
> **Three** dancers are hoping for the job.
> Three **talented** dancers are hoping for the job.
>
> I need **nine** laborers for the project.
> I need nine **strong and healthy** laborers for the project.

Quantifiers also describe quantities and amounts. Here are some of the most common:

a couple of	(a) few
a great deal of	(a) little
a lot of	many
all	much
any	no
both	several
each	some
every	

Quantifiers describe the number of the modified noun; accompanying adjectives describe the attributes.

A couple of **interesting** facts about him are in this book.

All **wealthy** nations should help the less fortunate ones.

John knows a few **hilarious** jokes.

Some **primitive** tribes once lived in this region.

EXERCISE
13·2

Write an original sentence using the determiner in parentheses and including a descriptive adjective. For example:

(two) *I'd like two crisp apples, please.*

1. (his) _____

2. (no) _____

3. (their) _____

4. (six) _____

5. (any) _____

6. (a great deal of) _____

7. (little) _____

8. (many) _____

9. (her) _____

10. (few) _____

11. (a few) _____

12. (many a) _____

13. (each) _____

14. (a lot of) _____

15. (thirty) _____

Often, more than one determiner can be used at a time, as with **a couple of, a great deal of, a lot of, a few,** and **a little.** Besides the indefinite article, the definite article and possessives can be used together with **all, both,** and **no.** For example:

> **The few** good friends he had were gone.
>
> **All the** children were finally asleep.
>
> **Both my** daughters have become ballerinas.
>
> I have **no more** money or time to give you.
>
> **Her many** kind deeds were remembered after her death.

Such and **what** are also determiners that can function alone or with another determiner. **So** cannot function alone and must be combined with another determiner. For example:

> They won't tolerate **such** behavior.
>
> Have you ever experienced **such an** exciting day?
>
> **What** happiness I feel today!
>
> **What little** time is left in the day I want to spend with you.
>
> There is **so much** work to do!

EXERCISE
13·3

Write an original sentence using the two determiners provided in parentheses. For example:

(so much) *John always has so much free time.*

1. (such a) _____

2. (both my) _____

3. (a lot of) _____

4. (no more) _____

5. (many a) _____

6. (so little) _____

7. (all the) _____

8. (a few) _____

9. (the few) _____

10. (a little) _____

It has already been pointed out that ordinal numbers can function as determiners. However, when they are combined with articles and demonstratives, they become nouns instead. For example:

NUMBER AS DETERMINER	NUMBER AS NOUN
Two boys began to cry.	**The two** of them began to cry.
Nine men are needed for the team.	**These nine** will make good team members.

Circle the letter of the word or phrase that best completes each sentence.

1. James asked for _____ new bicycle for his birthday.
   a. those   b. a   c. two   d. one's

2. Do you know the girls? Those _____ look like sisters.
   a. two   b. their   c. every   d. both

3. _____ rich uncle came for a visit.
   a. Our   b. All   c. More   d. A few

4. _____ happy moment was shared in their family.
   a. Some   b. So much   c. Much   d. Many a

5. Do you know _____ players out on the field?
   a. a little   b. what little   c. those   d. two of

6. _____ great sadness our village endured today!
   a. What   b. A little   c. So many   d. The few

7. Someone tried to burglarize our _____ neighbor's house.
   a. many   b. new   c. several   d. that

8. There are _____ problems in the world.
   a. a lot   b. any   c. so many   d. great deal of

9. Where are _____ wild animals?
   a. all the   b. the one   c. some of   d. no

10. _____ a wonderful evening it was!
    a. Much   b. So   c. Which   d. What

Adverbs of degree

The function of adverbs is to modify verbs, adjectives, and other adverbs. Some adverbs modify *the degree* of a verb's action, an adjective's description, or an adverb's description.

Here is a list of commonly used adverbs of degree. The *degrees of accomplishment* that they represent are described in the heading of each list of phrases.

Already achieved

completely

Recently achieved

just

Not yet achieved

almost
nearly

Strong degree of accomplishment

extremely
too
very/not very

Moderate degree of accomplishment
quite
rather

Mild degree of accomplishment
kind of
scarcely
somewhat
sort of

The adverbs **quite**, **rather**, **somewhat**, **too**, and **very/not very** modify adjectives and other adverbs rather than verbs. For example:

> The pups are still **quite** small.
>
> That's a **rather** skimpy dress you're wearing.
>
> It's **somewhat** chilly in here.
>
> He's **too** old for you.
>
> You look **very** healthy.
>
> I'm **not very** young anymore.

Adverbs of degree are most often placed before the verb, adjective, or adverb they modify. For example:

> **Verb:** We j**ust** moved to Los Angeles.
>
> **Adjective:** John has an **extremely** high fever.
>
> **Adverb:** It was a **very** quickly moving storm.

In a complex verb, the adverb of degree appears before the main verb: **I don't *quite* understand. I have *almost* completed the project.**

The adverb **enough** means *an adequate amount or degree* and is placed *after* an adjective or adverb.

> Is that coat large **enough** for you?
>
> She spoke slowly **enough** for me to understand her.
>
> That rope isn't strong **enough**.
>
> The ambulance didn't arrive soon **enough**.

If you place **enough** before a noun, it means *a sufficient amount* and becomes a determiner rather than an adverb:

> Do you have **enough** milk for the pancakes?

EXERCISE
13·5

Write original sentences using the phrase provided in parentheses.

1. (not very long) _____

2. (tall enough) _____

3. (rather unusual) _____

4. (somewhat vague) _____

5. (almost forgot) _____

6. (extremely intelligent) _____

7. (almost finished) _____

8. (just arrived) _____

9. (kind of old) _____

10. (hardly ready) _____

11. (too heavy) _____

12. (completely exhausted) _____

13. (nearly injured) _____

14. (scarcely alive) _____

15. (sort of sad) _____

Gerunds, infinitives, and participles

·14·

Gerunds

A gerund is a *verbal*, meaning it comes from a verb and resembles a present participle because it ends in **-ing**. It expresses a state of being or an action, but it does not function as a verb, but rather is used like a noun. Here is a comparison of present participles and gerunds to illustrate how they are used differently.

PRESENT PARTICIPLE	GERUND
Why is water **running** in the bathtub?	**Running** is a good form of exercise.
Tom was **singing** in the shower.	I heard **singing** in the other room.
They are **laughing** at his jokes.	Her stomach hurt from **laughing**.

Since a gerund is used like a noun, it can function in a sentence like other nouns. In the preceding examples, the gerunds were used as the subject of the sentence, the direct object, and the object of a preposition, respectively. These same sentences can be expressed with other nouns:

> **Subject**
> **Running** is a good form of exercise.
> **Tennis** is a good form of exercise.

> **Direct object**
> I heard **singing** in the other room.
> I heard **music** in the other room.

> **Object of a preposition**
> Her stomach hurt from **laughing**.
> Her stomach hurt from **the operation**.

Just like nouns, gerunds can be modified by determiners and adjectives. For example:

> **Your** arguing has to stop.
> **This constant** fighting is driving me mad.
> I heard **quiet** sighing on the other side of the door.

Since a gerund expresses a state of being or an action like a verb, it can be accompanied by an object just as a verb can. Compare the following pairs of sentences:

Verb: He **makes** fun of the younger boy.
Gerund: Making fun of the younger boy was very cruel.

Verb: She **took** violin lessons.
Gerund: She hated **taking** violin lessons.

EXERCISE 14·1

Replace the noun or phrase shown in bold with an appropriate gerund. For example:

The sound of her voice made me very sad.

Her weeping made me very sad.

1. **The war** made life in our school unbearable.

   _____

2. I like **a leisurely stroll** through the park.

   _____

3. **Funny stories** always amused the children.

   _____

4. He tries to keep in shape with **a regular workout**.

   _____

5. The unruly boy needed **discipline and guidance**.

   _____

6. The twins put on a lot of weight from **a diet of sweets**.

   _____

7. **The team's poor performance** put the fans in a bad mood.

   _____

8. Did you hear **that strange noise**?

   _____

9. **Your poor attitude** won't help to solve your problems.

   _____

10. I suppose I'm guilty of **a weird sense of humor**.

   _____

EXERCISE

14·2

Basing your answer on the statement provided, write an original sentence with the verb in bold expressed as a gerund. For example:

He **studied** the long text.

His studying of the long text helped him understand it better.

1. They constantly **bickered** about money.

   _____

2. I **returned** the books to the library.

   _____

3. Mom wasn't amused when Jim **broke** the vase.

   _____

4. The man **drank and ate** too much.

   _____

5. She **smiled**, but it didn't change her husband's anger.

   _____

Sometimes there is confusion about the use of a gerund or a present participle. Both can often be used in similar statements, but the meaning is different. Here is an example:

> Jim's constant **complaining** about the food was annoying. (*complaining = gerund*)
>
> Jim, constantly **complaining** about the food, was annoying. (*complaining = present participle*)

In the first sentence, it is *Jim's complaint about the food* that was annoying. In the second, *Jim himself* was annoying.

Notice that *Jim's* in the first example is a possessive. That is one clue that *complaining* is being used as a noun. Another clue is the modifier *constant*, which is used as an adjective. In the second sentence, *Jim* is the subject of the sentence and does not use the possessive. The phrase that follows tells about Jim; it is an adjectival phrase and modifies *Jim*. In that phrase, *constantly* is an adverb. It is the clue that *complaining* is not a noun but the present participle of the verb *complain*.

Here is another pair of sentences. Examine their parts carefully to determine why one sentence contains a gerund and the other a present participle.

> We listened to the woman's frantic **screaming**.
>
> We listened to the woman, frantically **screaming**.

In the first sentence, we listened to *the screaming*. In the second, we listened to *the frantically screaming woman*. The present participle *screaming* modifies *woman*.

Write two original sentences using the verb provided in parentheses. In one, use the verb as a gerund; in the other, use it as a present participle. The sentences do not have to be similar. For example:

(see)

Seeing the newborn pups brought a smile to her lips.

Mary, suddenly seeing her brother at the door, let out a scream of joy.

1. (hope)

_____

_____

2. (find)

_____

_____

3. (learn)

_____

_____

4. (help)

_____

_____

5. (attend)

_____

_____

Infinitives

Like gerunds, infinitives are verbals (derived from the infinitive form of verbs such as **to run, to have, to speak,** and so on) that are used as nouns and function quite easily as the subject of a sentence. For example:

> **To pretend** you're something you're not is foolish.
>
> **To be** on the basketball team was his fervent wish.

When infinitives are used as direct objects, care must be taken, because not all verbs can use an infinitive as their direct object. Here are some commonly used verbs that can have infinitives as direct objects:

agree	need
attempt	plan
decide	pretend
expect	promise
hope	want
learn	

Here are a few example sentences using these verbs:

> Jack decided **to buy** a new car.
> No one needs **to know** about our plan.
> Jean will want **to speak** to you about this.

EXERCISE 14·4

In the blank provided, write an infinitive or infinitive phrase using the verb in parentheses. For example:

(buy) *To buy a car now* might be a bad idea.

1. (marry) _____ won't bring you happiness.

2. (travel) _____ would take too long.

3. (speak) In Europe I learned _____.

4. (love) That woman only pretended _____.

5. (be) _____ is the only thing I ask of you.

After some verbs, both infinitives and gerunds can be used as direct objects. Some of these verbs are as follows:

begin	love
continue	remember
hate	start
like	try

For example:

> I begin **to worry** about him. I begin **worrying** about him.
> Why do you hate **to practice**? Why do you hate **practicing**?
> John tried **to help** them. John tried **helping** them.

Using the pairs of verbs in parentheses, write original sentences using an infinitive as the direct object. Write a second sentence with a gerund as the direct object wherever possible. For example:

(begin/speak)

I began to speak more politely to her.

I began speaking more politely to her.

1. (love/read)

_____

_____

2. (learn/play)

_____

_____

3. (continue/drive)

_____

_____

4. (remember/pay)

_____

_____

5. (like/swim)

_____

_____

The antonyms **remember** and **forget** can have either an infinitive or a gerund as their direct object. However, the meaning of such sentences will be quite different. For example:

Did you remember **to feed** the dog? (*Did you feed the dog?*)

Did you remember **feeding** the dog? (*Did you remember that you fed the dog? Or have you forgotten?*)

She forgot **to take** the chicken out of the freezer. (*She left the chicken in the freezer.*)

She forgot **taking** the chicken out of the freezer. (*She doesn't remember that she took the chicken out of the freezer.*)

Passive voice infinitives can function as nouns like other infinitives. The passive voice consists of a conjugated form of **be** plus a past participle.

PASSIVE VOICE SENTENCE	PASSIVE INFINITIVE
He **is being punished** for his actions.	to be punished
It **is being decided** by a court.	to be decided
Mary **is being given** a second chance.	to be given

Perfect tense infinitives are derived from the present or past perfect tense and are used as nouns like other infinitives. Passive voice sentences can form perfect tense infinitives as well.

PERFECT TENSE SENTENCE	PERFECT TENSE INFINITIVE
She **has found** her little brother.	to have found
I **had bought** her a gift.	to have bought
He **has been arrested** for the crime.	to have been arrested
We **had been searched** by the police.	to have been searched

Here are some examples of passive infinitives and perfect tense infinitives used as nouns:

To be punished for something I didn't do is unfair.
To be called a liar was the greatest insult.

To have broken your promise to me is unforgiveable.
To have spent all your savings was a grave mistake.

To have been accused of a crime was the final humiliation.
To have been fired so suddenly came as a shock to me.

EXERCISE
14·6

Rewrite the sentence making the phrase in bold an infinitive. The sentence does not have to reflect the same meaning as the original. For example:

He **is being taken** out of the country.

To be taken out of the country was not what she wanted.

1. They **have been fined** for speeding.

   _____

2. I **have lived** in America.

   _____

3. Martin **has achieved** great success.

   _____

4. Laura **had been selected** to head the committee.

_____

5. The men **are being fired** by the new manager.

_____

Participles

Both present and past participles can function as modifiers. They can act as a single adjective or in an adjectival phrase. For example:

> **Running** water is a luxury in this village.
> The boy, **running in fear of his life**, bolted into the church.

> The **broken** lamp is beyond repair.
> His right leg, **painfully broken in a fall from the roof**, will require surgery.

A present participle used as an adjective is much like a replacement for a verb in a relative clause.

PRESENT PARTICIPLE	RELATIVE CLAUSE
running water	water, **which is running**
sleeping children	children, **who are sleeping**
flowering rosebushes	rosebushes, **which are flowering**

A past participle used as an adjective is much like a replacement for a relative clause with a passive voice verb.

PAST PARTICIPLE	PASSIVE RELATIVE CLAUSE
a broken window	a window, **which has been broken**
the wounded soldier	the soldier, **who has been wounded**
stolen money	money, **which has been stolen**

EXERCISE
14·7

Write four original sentences for each verb. Change the verb to a present participle and then a past participle, and use each as a single adjective and in an adjectival phrase. For example:

(break)

The sound of breaking glass scared us.

The window, breaking from the force of the wind, crashed to the floor.

A broken finger was the only injury she suffered.

The egg, broken open by the gentle pecking of the chick, soon revealed the newborn bird.

1. (return)

2. (punish)

3. (recruit)

4. (follow)

5. (insult)

Auxiliaries

Three of the most common auxiliarics arc **have**, **shall**, and **will**. A conjugated form of **have** with an accompanying past participle is used to form the present and past perfect tenses, and **shall** and **will** are used with an accompanying infinitive to form the future and future perfect tenses. Here are some examples:

> **Present perfect:** My brother **has** been working in Boston.
>
> **Past perfect:** Ms. Ramirez **had** spent several hours at the mall.
>
> **Future: Shall** we go into the living room?
>
> **Future perfect:** They **will** have traveled more than a thousand miles by next week.

Many English speakers avoid using **shall**. This comes in part from its use in a contraction (*I shall* = *I'll*), which sounds and looks like a contraction formed with **will** (*I will* = *I'll*). **Shall** is most frequently used with the first person singular and plural pronouns (*I* and *we*) but is replaced by **will** in casual language.

> I **shall** try to spend more time with you. I **will** try to spend more time with you.
>
> We **shall** be traveling by train. We **will** be traveling by train.

In a question formed with **I** or **we** as the subject, the use of **shall** cannot be avoided if the question is to make sense. The use of **will** is also correct, but the meaning is quite different. For example:

> **Shall** we go out to dinner tonight? (*A suggestion of what to do tonight*)
>
> **Will** we go out to dinner tonight? (*A question about possible dinner plans for tonight*)
>
> **Shall** I lend you my car for the day? (*A suggestion to lend you my car*)
>
> **Will** I lend you my car for the day? (*A question about my plan to lend you my car*)

When negated with **not**, these auxiliaries can become contractions, as in the following instances:

> have not = haven't   has not = hasn't   had not = hadn't
>
> shall not = shan't
>
> will not = won't

Rewrite each present tense sentence in the specified perfect and future tenses.

1. John is at work.

   PRESENT PERFECT _____

   PAST PERFECT _____

   FUTURE _____

2. Do I visit you often?

   PRESENT PERFECT _____

   PAST PERFECT _____

   FUTURE _____

3. He is speaking for two hours.

   PRESENT PERFECT _____

   PAST PERFECT _____

   FUTURE _____

   FUTURE PERFECT _____

4. The little boy breaks the vase.

   PRESENT PERFECT _____

   PAST PERFECT _____

   FUTURE _____

   FUTURE PERFECT _____

5. Does she help out in the kitchen?

   PRESENT PERFECT _____

   PAST PERFECT _____

   FUTURE _____

Should and would

The auxiliaries **should** and **would** are the past tense forms of **shall** and **will** and are used very much as they are. That means that **should** is used with the first person singular and plural pronouns but is often replaced by **would**. One of their common uses is in *indirect discourse*. When reporting what someone has said, the verb phrase in the quoted line includes **should** or **would**. For example:

> **Direct discourse:** John says, "I will help Mary with the cleaning."
> **Indirect discourse:** John said that he **would** help Mary with the cleaning.
>
> **Direct discourse:** John says, "You will have a good time there."
> **Indirect discourse:** John said that I **should/would** have a good time there.
>
> **Direct discourse:** John says, "They will be driving through the Alps."
> **Indirect discourse:** John said that they **would** be driving through the Alps.

Should is often used to suggest an action. Any pronoun can be the subject of **should** in such sentences.

> I **should** stay home and relax tonight.
> You **shouldn't** watch so much television.
> Perhaps he **should** wear a warmer coat.

In conditional sentences, in which a result will occur if certain conditions are met, both **should** and **would** are used, although there is a tendency to use **would** most often.

Condition	Result

> If you saved more, you **would** have plenty of money for retirement.
> If my brother were here, he **would** know what to advise me.
> If we saw Uncle Henry, we **should/would** speak to him.

It is possible for the clause that expresses the result to precede the one that sets the condition.

> You **would** have plenty of money for retirement if you saved more.

Should have and would have

Should have is used with an accompanying past participle to express *what outcome was preferred but did not occur.* For example:

> You **should have** driven more carefully. (*The preferred outcome was having driven more carefully, but that did not occur.*)
> I **should have** brought an umbrella. (*The preferred outcome of having an umbrella handy did not occur.*)

Would have is used with an accompanying past participle in conditional sentences to express an action in the past. For example:

> The man **would have** felt better if he had taken his medicine.
> If I had known you liked candy, I **would have** brought you some pralines.

*In the blank provided, write the correct verb form: **should, would, should have,** or **would have**. If two answers are possible, provide both. For example:*

He <u>should have</u> known better than to lie to Father.

1. If you were better prepared, you _____ pass the test.

2. _____ you go out in such a light jacket?

3. Michael and Laura _____ gone to New York by plane.

4. We _____ probably head for home soon.

5. Bill _____ carried the heavy box if he had been at home.

6. Someone _____ told me about this situation.

7. If Uncle Samuel had remembered his glasses, he _____ been able to read the signs.

8. I warned you about coming home late. You _____ been home by eleven.

9. _____ I open the blinds, or do you prefer to do it yourself?

10. If the storm had ended sooner, we _____ continued on the hike.

11. Why _____ I pay for this? I didn't order it.

12. She _____ worn her raincoat. Now she'll get soaked to the skin.

13. I _____ borrowed the money for her tuition.

14. Jane _____ made some sandwiches if she had been told about the picnic.

15. It's Mom's birthday. We _____ bought her a gift and a card.

Modals

The modal auxiliary verbs come in a variety of forms. Some include verbs that can be conjugated, and others consist of a single verb form that cannot be conjugated. In addition, not all modal auxiliaries can be used in all tenses. Here are some commonly used modal auxiliary verbs in their present and past tense forms.

PRESENT TENSE	PAST TENSE
can	could
have got to, has got to	had got to
have to, has to	had to
may	might
must	—
—	had better
need, needs	needed
ought to	—

Modals such as these are accompanied by infinitives. As explained in Chapter 14, infinitives can be a single verb or a passive infinitive. Note that some modals consist of a phrase ending in **to.** That *particle word* is always part of the modal. The following are some examples:

ACTIVE VOICE SENTENCES	PASSIVE VOICE SENTENCES
He **can** hold his breath for a long time.	They **needed to** be located soon.
Why **must** you shout at me?	We **have to** be protected from him.
May I come in?	It **has got to** be decided today.
You **had better** feed that hungry dog.	**Could** our house be built over there?

A few modal auxiliaries have an alternative form:

MODAL AUXILIARY	ALTERNATIVE MODAL AUXILIARY
can	be able to
must	have to
shall/will	be going to
should	be supposed to

These alternative modals can replace the regular modals.

I **can** understand what you mean.	I **am able to** understand what you mean.
We **must** help our neighbors.	We **have to** help our neighbors.
He **will** buy a few gifts at the mall.	He **is going to** buy a few gifts at the mall.
She **should** rest more often.	She **is supposed to** rest more often.

The alternative modal auxiliaries come in handy when using tenses other than the present or past tense, because some modals are limited to certain tenses. The following examples show three modals and how their alternative form can be used in various tenses.

MODAL AUXILIARY	ALTERNATE MODAL AUXILIARY
Present: I can work harder.	I am able to work harder.
Past: I could work harder.	I was able to work harder.
Present perfect: —	I have been able to work harder.
Past perfect: —	I had been able to work harder.
Future: —	I shall be able to work harder.
Present: We must hurry.	We have to hurry.
Past: —	We had to hurry.
Present perfect: —	We have had to hurry.
Past perfect: —	We had had to hurry.
Future: —	We shall have to hurry.
Present: —	You are supposed to stay home.
Past: You should stay home.	You were supposed to stay home.
Present perfect: —	You have been supposed to stay home.
Past perfect: —	You had been supposed to stay home.
Future: —	You will be supposed to stay home.

When verb phrases become too complex and sound awkward, there is a tendency to use a simpler phrase. For example:

Complex: You had been supposed to stay home.

Simpler: You were supposed to stay home.

EXERCISE
15·3

Change the sentence provided by adding the modal auxiliaries shown in parentheses. Retain the tense of the original sentence. If the modal does not exist in the given tense, use its alternative form. For example:

James has spoken with her.

(must) *James has had to speak with her.*

1. My daughter learned a funny poem.

   (can) _____

   (be supposed to) _____

   (have to) _____

2. Will you be home for supper?

   (must) _____

   (can) _____

   (be going to) _____

3. Someone helps the man with his luggage.

   (ought to) _____

   (need to) _____

   (have got to) _____

4. Jack trains for the marathon.

   (must) _____

   (be able to) _____

   (be supposed to) _____

5. The officer stamped my passport.

   (may) _____

   (be supposed to) _____

   (can) _____

Modals and past participles

Just like **should have** and **would have**, some modal auxiliary verbs can be combined with **have** and accompanied by a past participle. The use of this form of auxiliary changes the *nuance* of the sentence's meaning. For example:

> He **could have** heard me. (*He had the ability to hear me. It was likely that he heard me.*)
>
> He **may have** heard me. (*It is possible that he heard me.*)
>
> He **might have** heard me. (*There was a slight possibility that he heard me, but he probably did not.*)
>
> He **must have** heard me. (*I assume that he heard me.*)
>
> He **ought to have** heard me. (*It's a pity that he did not hear me.*)

Here are a few more examples. Study them and determine what the nuance of meaning is in each.

> Jack could have grilled a couple of steaks.
>
> Jack may have grilled a couple of steaks.
>
> Jack might have grilled a couple of steaks.
>
> Jack must have grilled a couple of steaks.
>
> Jack ought to have grilled a couple of steaks.

EXERCISE 15·4

Rewrite each sentence in the missing tenses, using alternative modal forms where necessary.

1. PRESENT Ms. Gupta needs to get some sleep.

   PAST _____

   PRESENT PERFECT _____

   FUTURE _____

2. PRESENT _____

   PAST No one could help the poor man.

   PRESENT PERFECT _____

   FUTURE _____

3. PRESENT _____

   PAST _____

   PRESENT PERFECT Jim has had to be hospitalized.

   FUTURE _____

4. PRESENT _____

   PAST _____

   PRESENT PERFECT _____

   FUTURE Martin will not be able to go with you.

5. PRESENT He has to take the train to Seattle.

PAST _____

PRESENT PERFECT _____

FUTURE _____

Complete each sentence with any appropriate phrase. For example:

She could have *attended the same university as Joe.*

1. I must have _____.

2. The other girls may have _____.

3. Karen might have _____.

4. You ought to have _____.

5. Should you have _____?

6. My mother never would have _____.

7. _____ forgotten about the party tonight.

8. _____ lost my keys.

9. _____ put your money in the bank.

10. _____ misunderstood me.

Using *get*

The verb **get** is used in a large variety of ways, a fact that can cause confusion for many people learning English, because that variety gives the verb numerous meanings. **Get** is an irregular verb and is conjugated as follows:

Present tense: he gets/he is getting

Past tense: he got/he was getting

Present perfect: he has gotten/he has been getting

Future tense: he will get/he will be getting

Perhaps the most common meanings of **get** are *become* and *receive*. In this instance, *become* is synonymous with *turn* (as in *The leaves are turning red*) rather than with *prepare for a profession* (such as *become a doctor*). When it means *become*, **get** is an intransitive verb. When it means *receive*, it is a transitive verb and can be accompanied by direct objects. **Get** can be used as an intransitive or a transitive verb as its meaning changes. Here are some example sentences:

GET MEANING *BECOME*	GET MEANING *RECEIVE*
It **gets** dark early in the winter.	Did you **get** my letter?
It **got** so cold last night.	Tom **got** a gift from his girlfriend.
The sky is **getting** bright.	I can't **get** money out of this ATM.

Another two meanings of **get** are *arrive* and *earn*. The former is an intransitive verb, and the latter is a transitive verb. For example:

GET MEANING *ARRIVE*	GET MEANING *EARN*
Marie will **get** home tomorrow.	I will be **getting** $11 an hour.
How do I **get** to State Street?	My cousin **got** a four-year scholarship.
She **got** to the station on foot.	You will **get** a reward for your heroism.

Rewrite each sentence in the tenses given.

1. PRESENT How do you get over that river?

   PAST _____

   PRESENT PERFECT _____

   FUTURE _____

2. PRESENT _____

   PAST The weather got very chilly again.

   PRESENT PERFECT _____

   FUTURE _____

3. PRESENT _____

   PAST _____

   PRESENT PERFECT She hasn't been getting all her pay.

   FUTURE _____

4. PRESENT _____

   PAST _____

   PRESENT PERFECT _____

   FUTURE We will get high marks for our science project.

Two more meanings of **get** are *have something done* and *take someone someplace*. For example:

GET MEANING *HAVE SOMETHING DONE*	GET MEANING *TAKE SOMEONE SOMEPLACE*
I have to **get** my hair cut.	I can **get** you to St. Louis by 10 p.m.
She **got** a beautiful dress made in Paris.	Jim **got** his girlfriend home on time.
I'll **get** the car repaired tomorrow.	We're **getting** you to the hospital right now.

Another pair of meanings comprises *understand* and *obtain* or *bring back*. For example:

GET MEANING *UNDERSTAND*	GET MEANING *OBTAIN/BRING BACK*
I didn't **get** his joke.	Please **get** me the scissors from that drawer.
She **got** my meaning but didn't like it.	John **got** some groceries this morning.
Don't you **get** it? They're angry with you.	Can you **get** my pills from the drugstore?

Two additional meanings are *have the opportunity* and *take transportation*. For example:

GET MEANING *HAVE THE OPPORTUNITY*	GET MEANING *TAKE TRANSPORTATION*
I hope I **get** to see the game on Friday.	We need to **get** the next bus.
Susan never **got** to take ballet lessons.	I **got** a flight to Memphis.
Tomorrow we **get** to go to the zoo.	If he had **gotten** the train, he'd be there by now.

EXERCISE
16·2

*Based on the description provided, write two original sentences using **get** in any tense that is appropriate.*

1. (have something done)

_____

_____

2. (take someone someplace)

_____

_____

3. (understand)

_____

_____

4. (obtain/bring back)

_____

_____

5. (have the opportunity)

_____

_____

6. (take transportation)

_____

_____

7. (receive)

_____

_____

8. (become)

_____

_____

9. (arrive)

_____

_____

10. (earn)

_____

_____

Passive voice

In colloquial language, the auxiliary **be** is sometimes replaced by **get** in a passive voice structure. **Get** is accompanied by a past participle, and the sentence's meaning resembles that of a passive voice sentence with the auxiliary **be**.

PASSIVE VOICE	PASSIVE VOICE WITH *GET*
The house **is** destroyed by a fire.	The house **gets** destroyed by a fire.
The boy was **being** punished.	The boy was **getting** punished.
The thief will **be** sentenced to 10 years.	The thief will **get** sentenced to 10 years.

As explained in Chapter 6, a passive voice structure can be introduced by other auxiliaries. The same occurs when **get** is part of that structure. For example:

He **wants** to **be** paid for his labors.
He **wants** to **get** paid for his labors.

EXERCISE
16·3

*Rewrite each sentence by changing the auxiliary **be** to a comparable form of **get**.*

1. The car is being repaired by a new mechanic.

_____

2. Was he promoted by Mr. Jackson?

_____

3. You will be rewarded for your service to the community.

_____

4. Ashley is kissed by Jim.

_____

5. I have often been massaged for my sore back.

_____

6. Does Mom like to be pampered on Mother's Day?

_____

7. She never wanted to be elected governor.

_____

8. The team will be trained by Coach Henderson.

_____

9. Was the dog being maltreated?

_____

10. Many citizens were being robbed in that neighborhood.

_____

EXERCISE
16·4

*Write an original passive voice sentence using **get** and the participle provided in parentheses. Use any tense that is appropriate. For example:*

(punished) *The boy will get punished for his bad behavior.*

1. (built) _____

2. (fed) _____

3. (painted) _____

4. (inflated) _____

5. (driven) _____

EXERCISE
16·5

Circle the letter of the word or phrase that best completes each sentence.

1. It seems to _____ hotter every summer.
   a. get
   b. getting
   c. qot
   d. has gotten

2. I don't get _____.
   a. some reasons
   b. that joke
   c. he is singing
   d. been punished

3. Why is he _____?
   a. got the messages from us
   b. gets a little lazy
   c. get it from us
   d. getting so angry

4. We just couldn't get _____ in time.
   a. from the officer
   b. for him
   c. of city hall
   d. to the train

5. I have been getting _____.
   a. a lot of postcards from them
   b. school by ten o'clock
   c. gone to the store
   d. reward for my son

6. She has no idea how to get _____.
   a. to Newark Airport
   b. bus station by two
   c. broken by the child
   d. it is funny

7. We need _____.
   a. to get him to the emergency room
   b. getting a loan from the bank
   c. get aboard the ship
   d. have gotten better seats

8. It's not fair that he gets _____.
   a. write several letters
   b. sending a fax or an e-mail
   c. more pay than Marie
   d. being so ill

9. I hope you _____.
   a. haven't gotten yet
   b. get to visit the aquarium
   c. to get a little more money
   d. getting a good impression of us

10. The old horse was _____ by the driver.
   a. got fed once a day
   b. getting beaten
   c. gets to graze in the pasture
   d. gotten lame and blind

Restrictive and nonrestrictive relative clauses

English relative clauses follow distinct patterns, some of which differ from the patterns in European languages. These are the relative pronouns used in relative clauses:

ANIMATE	INANIMATE
that	that
who	which
whom	
whose	whose, of which

The choice of using an animate or inanimate relative pronoun depends on the *antecedent* of the relative pronoun (the word to which the pronoun refers). If the antecedent is animate, it takes an animate relative pronoun; if it is inanimate, it takes an inanimate relative pronoun. For example:

> My brother, **who** is serving in the army right now, wants to become a teacher.
>
> My car, **which** is the latest Ford model, gets only average gas mileage.

When using a possessive relative pronoun with an inanimate antecedent, either **whose** or **of which** is correct.

> The factory, **whose** employees may be laid off, was built more than 50 years ago.
>
> The factory, the employees **of which** may be laid off, was built more than 50 years ago.

Combining sentences

It is possible to combine two sentences that share a common element—a noun or pronoun. One of those elements can be changed to a relative pronoun, and the two sentences can be written as one. The relative pronoun uses the same case (subjective, objective, or possessive) as the element that is changed. For example:

> Two sentences: The manager usually comes in late. I met **the manager** in Los Angeles.
>
> Combined sentence: The manager, **whom** I met in Los Angeles, usually comes in late.

Because **manager** is the direct object in the second of the two original sentences, the objective form **whom** is used as the relative pronoun in the combined sentence.

Prepositions

When a noun used as an indirect object is changed to a relative pronoun, the prepositions **to** or **for** usually introduce the relative pronoun. For example:

> The girl is sad. I give **the girl** some candy.
>
> The girl, **to whom** I give some candy, is sad.

> The boy attends our school. We buy **the boy** school supplies.
>
> The boy, **for whom** we buy school supplies, attends our school.

If a noun is the object of a preposition and is changed to a relative pronoun, the preposition will introduce the relative pronoun in the relative clause. For example:

> The house is too small. My family is supposed to live in **the house**.
>
> The house, **in which** my family is supposed to live, is too small.

EXERCISE 17·1

*Combine each pair of sentences by making the word in bold the relative pronoun. Make the second sentence the relative clause. Use only a form of **who** or **which**, and set off the relative clause with commas. For example:*

The men want to go on strike. **The men** used to get a good salary.

The men, who used to get a good salary, want to go on strike.

1. The boy is looking for his dog. **The boy** is one of my students.

   _____

2. Mr. Simmons moved here from Canada. **Mr. Simmons** has two daughters.

   _____

3. The woman is learning Spanish. Bob sent **the woman** several e-mails.

   _____

4. This room will serve as our family room. The dimensions of **the room** are 15 × 20 feet.

   _____

5. The new airport is located outside of town. **The new airport** has three terminals.

   _____

6. The head of the school became quite ill. We recently visited **the head of the school**.

   _____

7. Jack is a student at Harvard. **Jack's** parents are neighbors of mine.

   _____

8. Their children rarely argue. Tom bought **their children** computer games.

_____

9. Professor Hall is getting on in years. Jenny spoke with **Professor Hall** yesterday.

_____

10. The bed is brand-new. Their baby slept comfortably on **the bed**.

_____

Restrictive relative clauses

Restrictive relative clauses *define* or *limit* their antecedent. In such clauses, the relative pronoun is most often **that** and can replace either animate or inanimate nouns. These clauses are *not* set off by commas. Here are some examples:

> My sister **that works in Toledo** is a lawyer.

The antecedent **My sister** is defined as working in Toledo. The sentence implies that I have another sister that works elsewhere. For example:

> And my sister **that works in Denver** is a homemaker.

Here is another example:

> The books **that I bought yesterday** were on sale.

The antecedent **The books** is defined by when I bought them—**yesterday**. The sentence implies that I bought other books at another time. For example:

> And the books **that I bought this afternoon** were full price.

The relative pronoun **that** is universal, meaning it can be used with any antecedent in restrictive relative clauses. But **who, whom, whose,** and **which** can also be used in restrictive clauses. However, care must be taken to ensure that the relative clause really defines and limits the antecedent. Here are some examples:

> The elderly man **that** I met at your party paid me a call yesterday.
> The elderly man **whom** I met at your party paid me a call yesterday.

> The animals **that** are housed in the Jungle Building do not like cold weather.
> The animals **which** are housed in the Jungle Building do not like cold weather.

> The little boy **that** threw the rock ran around the corner of that house.
> The little boy **who** threw the rock ran around the corner of that house.

Rewrite each sentence by changing the relative pronoun **that** *to* **who, whom,** *or* **which.**

1. The film that is playing right now is very suspenseful.

   _____

2. His children that live in Chicago reside on the same street.

   _____

3. The teacher that I saw in the park is Ms. Garcia.

   _____

4. Is the woman that bought your house from Ireland?

   _____

5. The flowers that I bought for Jane are already wilting.

   _____

Earlier in this chapter, it was stated that a preposition should precede a relative pronoun in a relative clause. This is not the case if that clause is restrictive. In restrictive relative clauses, the preposition becomes the last element in the clause. For example:

> The actor **that** I spoke **of** is right over there.
>
> That is the man **that** I drove to Phoenix **with**.

You cannot say or write "**with that** I drove to Phoenix."

There is a simple rule that says a preposition should not end a sentence. If you were to follow that rule all the time, you would sometimes find yourself making awkward and odd-sounding statements. Even the legendary prime minister of Great Britain, Winston Churchill, found that rule lacking. When an editor rewrote a sentence in one of Churchill's papers to avoid ending a sentence with a preposition, Churchill supposedly wrote in reply, "This is the sort of bloody nonsense up with which I will not put."

The point is that a preposition can and often must end a sentence as illustrated earlier. Here are a few more examples where a preposition is at the end of a sentence:

> That's the uncle that I told you **about**.
>
> Is that the café that we ate **in**?
>
> Where is the pillow that the cat was sitting **on**?

When a restrictive relative clause uses the relative pronoun **that** as a direct object, indirect object, or object of a preposition, *the relative pronoun can be omitted.*

> **Direct object:** The hat I bought in Paris was crushed in my suitcase. (*The hat that I bought . . .*)
>
> **Indirect object:** The woman I gave the money to was most grateful. (*The woman that I gave . . .*)
>
> **Object of preposition:** The waiter she complained about had spilled water on her. (*The waiter that she complained . . .*)

Compose sentences with restrictive relative clauses using **that**. *The relative pronoun of the clause should conform to the description provided in parentheses. If the relative pronoun is in the objective case, write the sentence a second time, omitting the relative pronoun* **that**. *For example:*

(subject) *That is the student that lives in the new dormitory.*

(direct object) *Did you meet the lawyer that Mr. Brown hired?*

Did you meet the lawyer Mr. Brown hired?

1. (subject) _____

2. (direct object) _____

_____

3. (indirect object) _____

_____

4. (object of preposition) _____

_____

5. (subject) _____

6. (direct object) _____

_____

7. (indirect object) _____

_____

8. (object of preposition) _____

_____

9. (direct object) _____

_____

10. (object of preposition) _____

_____

Nonrestrictive relative clauses

Nonrestrictive relative clauses do not define or limit the antecedent. They provide *additional, parenthetical information*. Such clauses are always set off with commas, and prepositions precede the relative pronoun, particularly in formal style. These are the kind of relative clauses that were written in Exercise 17-1. Let's look at a few more examples of nonrestrictive relative clauses and how they differ in meaning from restrictive clauses.

> **Restrictive:** The boy **that** threw a rock at my window is hiding over there.
>
> **Nonrestrictive:** The boy, **who** threw a rock at my window, is hiding over there.

In the sentence with the restrictive relative clause, the speaker is identifying the boy. Apparently, the boy threw the rock at the window relatively recently. But in the sentence with the nonrestrictive relative clause, the speaker is pointing out where the boy is hiding and is adding the information that the boy threw a rock at his or her window. That could have happened a long time ago rather than recently.

Here is another example:

> **Restrictive:** The ladder **that** broke is lying next to the garage.
>
> **Nonrestrictive:** The ladder, **which** broke, is lying next to the garage.

In the sentence with the restrictive relative clause, someone apparently has more than one ladder, and one of them broke. But in the sentence with the nonrestrictive relative clause, the speaker is describing where the ladder is and adding the complaint that it broke.

It is often the speaker's or writer's prerogative to determine whether the meaning desired is restrictive or nonrestrictive. To determine whether the restrictive meaning is desired, ask, "Which one?"

> Which ladder? The ladder that broke.
>
> Which sister? The sister that lives in Toledo.
>
> Which woman? The woman I gave the money to.
>
> Which pillow? The pillow the cat was sitting on.

EXERCISE
17·4

Write two sentences for each phrase, using it first with a restrictive relative clause and then with a nonrestrictive one. Describe how the restrictive clause defines or limits its antecedent. For example:

(the new student)

The new student that lives on the third floor comes from India.

Other new students live on other floors.

The new student, who lives on the third floor, comes from India.

1. (our relatives) _____

_____

_____

2. (the landlord) _____

_____

_____

3. (three buildings) _____

_____

_____

4. (the contracts) _____

_____

_____

5. (my friend) _____

_____

_____

6. (the map) _____

_____

_____

7. (the best film) _____

_____

_____

8. (the country) _____

_____

_____

9. (the essay) _____

_____

_____

10. (the handsomest actor) _____

_____

_____

Coordinating and subordinating conjunctions

18

Coordinating conjunctions connect two independent clauses as one sentence. It is usual to separate the two clauses by a comma, but if the clauses are brief, the comma is sometimes omitted. The comma can also be omitted if the subject of the second clause is understood, because it is identical to the subject in the first clause. However, there are exceptions: **for** and **nor**. These conjunctions require a subject in both clauses.

The coordinating conjunctions are **and**, **but**, **for**, **nor**, **or**, **so**, and **yet**. The following are some examples of how these conjunctions are used.

And

The rain and frequent sunshine made the farmers happy, **and** the landscape responded with greenery and color. (*A subject in each independent clause*)

The farmers made their way into the fields **and** began the task of readying the soil for planting. (*Identical subject understood*)

But

One of the twins was certain that city life was for him, **but** the other quickly fled to a quiet village. (*A subject in each independent clause*)

The sisters loved to shop together **but** never saw each other at social gatherings. (*Identical subject understood*)

For

Young John rebelled against all authority, **for** his father had taught him that authority had its cruel side.

Nor

She never suggested she would marry him, **nor** did he give the impression that he was falling in love with her. (*A subject in each independent clause*)

Here, the verb in the second clause precedes the subject: *nor <u>did he</u> give the impression that he was falling in love with her.*

Or

Either you are taking money from the vault, **or** there is an invisible creature that has the combination. (*A subject in each independent clause*)

She either is a child prodigy **or** had musical training in another life. (*Identical subject understood*)

So

Aunt Vera is a wary driver, **so** it is no wonder that she avoids congested roads. (*A subject in each independent clause*)

Tom has a lot of problems with math **so** he spends many hours studying for exams. (*Identical subject understood*)

Yet

My son plays Bach with a master's touch, **yet** his favorite type of music is rap. (*A subject in each independent clause*)

The understudy practiced her lines at every free moment **yet** forgot nearly everything when she was finally onstage. (*Identical subject understood*)

EXERCISE 18·1

Complete each sentence with any appropriate clause. If a comma is not provided before a conjunction, assume that the subject in the second clause is understood and identical to the one in the first clause.

1. Jenny spent years in southern Texas, and _____.

2. We enjoyed our vacation in France, but _____.

3. _____, for the constant storms left the sea rough and dangerous.

4. Professor Hart neither berated his students nor _____.

5. Do you have vacation plans for the summer yet, or _____.

6. Mr. Willis hated driving his big car, so _____.

7. _____, yet I remember nothing that happened before the accident.

8. Someone will have to pay for the damage and _____.

9. _____ but lies around all day monitoring her Facebook page.

10. Jim hated parties and begging girls to dance with him, for _____.

11. My parents never told me about the birds and the bees, nor _____.

12. Maria is going to go to a private college or _____.

13. _____ so spends a lot of his time lifting weights.

14. Barbara made a long list of the guests she wanted to invite yet _____.

15. Ms. Hayes travels from city to city and _____.

The conjunctions **but** and **for** are also commonly used as prepositions. As a preposition, **but** means *except*. For example:

Everyone **but** Alex was invited to her party.

As a preposition, **for** means *as a benefit to* or *in favor of*. For example:

I have a special gift **for** my daughter.

Circle the letter of the word or phrase that best completes each sentence.

1. You are either going out of your mind, _____ you have no idea how serious this is.
   a. for   b. or   c. so   d. and

2. Mr. Carson has an apartment in the city _____ lives with his mother in the suburbs.
   a. but   b. for   c. nor   d. or

3. Doris avoids her former husband, for _____.
   a. was always afraid of his moods   c. spent all their money on gambling
   b. began drinking heavily   d. he has a mean streak in him

4. _____, yet you continue to waste your time playing golf.
   a. Either you don't like going to work   c. She is very interested in athletics
   b. You are such a talented programmer   d. They will join you on the green

5. _____, nor do I have any patience with your behavior.
   a. She does not understand you   c. You are behaving badly again
   b. I do not have the ability to control you   d. He will never come back to us

6. Mr. Garcia made an illegal turn left and _____.
   a. was issued a citation   c. no one saw the accident
   b. a policeman pulled him over   d. he realized he had made a mistake

7. It was hard for Laura to exaggerate the truth, _____.
   a. and Tom was willing to lie to her   c. for her parents had taught her not to lie
   b. but was comfortable with the story   d. or she tried not to lie to them

8. The man was badly injured _____ continued to struggle to get to safety.
   a. so   b. nor   c. or   d. yet

9. He fears large dogs, _____ it's understandable that he has no pets.
   a. so   b. nor   c. or   d. yet

10. You are neither a member of this family _____ a welcome guest.
    a. so   b. nor   c. or   d. yet

Subordinating conjunctions

Subordinating conjunctions introduce a dependent clause (one that *depends* on the accompanying independent clause to complete its meaning). If the subordinating clause precedes the independent clause, it is separated from the independent clause by a comma. If it follows the independent clause, a comma is not used.

The list of subordinating conjunctions is long. Here are some of the common ones:

after	once
although	since
as	that
as if	though
as though	till
because	unless

before	until
even though	when
if	whenever
in order that	where
now that	while

Compare the use or omission of a comma in the following pairs of sentences.

After Daniel bought everyone dinner, he discovered that he had only $6 left.
She spoke to me **as if** I didn't have a brain in my head.

Because you have shown such bravery, the mayor wishes to present you with a medal.
I spend time at Pearl Harbor **whenever** I visit Honolulu.

Unless you start coming to work on time, you will soon be without a job.
John started dinner **while** his wife was putting the baby to bed.

EXERCISE
18·3

Complete each sentence with any appropriate phrase.

1. While _____, I went out to the garage to wash the car.

2. If _____, you're going to get a ticket for speeding.

3. Tears welled up in my eyes whenever _____.

4. Before I bought a new suit, _____.

5. Although _____, she can run as fast as the tallest girl.

6. Now that _____, you have my permission to drive the car alone.

7. _____ unless you start doing some serious studying.

8. Until I met Maria, _____.

9. As I told you in my recent letter, _____.

10. Although _____, I will try to pay my rent on time.

The conjunction *as*

As is sometimes confused with **like**, but the two words are used differently. **As** is a subordinating conjunction and introduces a dependent clause. **Like** is a preposition and introduces a prepositional phrase. Despite this difference, some people try to use **like** as a conjunction. For example:

Incorrect: Like my father always said, you have to be smart to stay smart.
Correct: As my father always said, you have to be smart to stay smart.

Incorrect: Like we did as children, we loved to play Monopoly.
Correct: As we did as children, we loved to play Monopoly.

Here are some examples in which **like** is used correctly as a preposition:

Everyone says my daughter looks **like** me.

My cake doesn't taste **like** your cake.

Write three original sentences using **as** as a conjunction. Then write two original sentences using **like** as a preposition.

As

1. _____

2. _____

3. _____

Like

4. _____

5. _____

The conjunction *that*

The conjunction **that** is used a bit differently from other subordinating conjunctions. It connects the verb in the introductory clause with the dependent clause. If the meaning of the sentence is not altered and the sentence does not sound awkward, **that** is often omitted but understood. For example:

My boss suggested **that** I take some time off to rest.

My boss suggested I take some time off to rest.

Did anyone tell him **that** his wife had won the lottery?

Did anyone tell him his wife had won the lottery?

No one knew **that** Ms. Olson had been promoted to vice president.

No one knew Ms. Olson had been promoted to vice president.

Write five pairs of original sentences with the conjunction **that**. Include **that** in the first sentence and omit it in the second. For example:

John hoped that his wife would feel better soon.

John hoped his wife would feel better soon.

1. _____

_____

2. _____

3. _____

4. _____

5. _____

The conjunction *because*

Some grammarians suggest that the conjunction **because** should not be used to introduce a sentence. However, many people ignore this idea, and it is used extensively by English speakers and writers. But care must be taken with long clauses, for there seems to be a tendency to leave the dependent clause as a *fragment*. For example:

> **Incorrect: Because** technology and widespread communications have made life throughout the globe so comfortable. (*Lacking an independent clause*)

> **Correct: Because** technology and widespread communications have made life throughout the globe so comfortable, some experts believe that human beings are losing their creative abilities.

Of course, **because** can begin the dependent clause that follows the independent clause. For example:

> We have to change how we use fossil fuel **because** the world's oil will someday be used up.

EXERCISE
18·6

Write five original sentences with the subordinating conjunction **because**.

1. _____

2. _____

3. _____

4. _____

5. _____

Phrasal verbs

19

Phrasal verbs are verbs combined with adverbs and prepositions to make a completely new meaning from that of the original verb. For example, when the verb **put** is combined with **up** and **with**, the original meaning of **put** (*place*) is lost, and a new meaning is created (*endure*).

> I cannot **put up with** your bad behavior. = I cannot **endure** your bad behavior.

Chapter 17 highlighted the phrasal verb **put up with** in a comment about how Winston Churchill mocked someone's attempt to avoid putting a preposition at the end of a sentence: "This is the sort of bloody nonsense up with which I will not put." Attempts to follow the rule that prepositions may not end a sentence will end in failure when it comes to phrasal verbs. That is because certain prepositions are used as *adverbs* (sometimes referred to as *particles*) when part of a phrasal verb. That is actually the use of **up** in the phrasal verb **put up with**. Churchill's sentence should have ended with the preposition **up**, which is used as an adverb: "This is the sort of bloody nonsense with which I will not put up."

Let's look at how other adverbs and prepositions further change the meaning of **put**.

put down

1. *ridicule* or *demean someone or something* = You always **put** me **down**. Don't I do anything that pleases you?
2. *write* = **Put down** every word that is said in the meeting.

put down for

register someone to participate in an activity = Mary loves soccer. You can **put** her **down for** that.

put on

1. *pretend* = He's not really sick. He's just **putting on**.
2. *tease, joke* = Bill won the lottery? I don't believe it! You're **putting** me **on**!

The list of phrasal verbs is very long; therefore this chapter will deal only with some of the most common ones. Dictionaries with a complete list of phrasal verbs are readily available and can serve as useful resources.

The following sections show how other verbs change their meaning as phrasal verbs and how they are used.

Be

be on *or* be off

an apparatus or machine is functioning (**on**) *or has stopped functioning* (**off**) = Is your computer **on**? I want to check my e-mails.
Why **is** the TV **off**? I want to watch the news.

be in *or* be out

available at home or at the office (**in**) *or away from home or the office* (**out**) = Will Dr. Smith **be in** today? I need to speak with him.
You **were out** all night. Where were you?

be up to

1. *have the ability or strength to do something* = I'm tired. **I'm** not **up to** one of Bob's parties tonight.
2. *suspicious, having evil intentions* = There's a man hiding in the shadows. I think **he's up to** no good.

be onto

having an important idea or clue for solving a problem = What a great invention! **You're** really **onto** something!

Check

check in(to)

record one's arrival = When I got to the hotel, I **checked in** at the reception desk. Then I **checked into** my room.

check on

investigate the status of someone or something = We need to **check on** our flight's departure time.

check in on *or* check up on

investigate the condition of someone or something = I went to **check in on** Ms. Brown to see whether she was feeling better. Jane **checks up on** her grandmother twice a week.

Do

do over

repeat = That paint job looks awful. You'll have to **do** it **over**.

Figure

figure in(to)

be included = The idea of children doesn't **figure in(to)** the couple's plans.

figure out

learn or understand = Did you finally **figure out** the answer to that question?

Rewrite each sentence in the missing tenses.

1. PRESENT Those boys are up to something dangerous.

   PAST _____

   PRESENT PERFECT _____

   FUTURE _____

2. PRESENT _____

   PAST We checked Into our motel around sunset.

   PRESENT PERFECT _____

   FUTURE _____

3. PRESENT _____

   PAST _____

   PRESENT PERFECT I have done the entire assignment over again.

   FUTURE _____

4. PRESENT _____

   PAST _____

   PRESENT PERFECT _____

   FUTURE Will she figure out the solution?

5. PRESENT How do you put up with their bickering?

   PAST _____

   PRESENT PERFECT _____

   FUTURE _____

Fill in the blank with the word that best completes each sentence. Choose from the phrasal verbs previously illustrated. For example:

It's hard to put _up_ with her crying.

1. The dentist is _____ but will return tomorrow at eight.

2. A trip to Orlando doesn't _____ into our vacation plans.

3. I just can't _____ with his laziness and bad manners.

4. I think you're really _____ the answer to this problem!

Phrasal verbs   151

5. Go to the family room and _____ up on the children.

6. I plugged the radio in, but it's still _____.

7. This is so difficult. I'll never figure it _____.

8. It's embarrassing. Why do you _____ me down in front of people?

9. You can _____ into your room after 2 p.m.

10. The Joneses never seem to _____ in when I come by for a visit.

Many phrasal verbs that have an adverb (particle) in the phrase can put the adverb in two different positions: one before the object of the verb and the other after the object of the verb. For example:

> Did you figure **out** the answer?
> Did you figure the answer **out**?

> The stenographer put **down** his testimony in shorthand.
> The stenographer put his testimony **down** in shorthand.

If the object of the phrasal verb is a pronoun, the adverb follows the object.

> Did you figure it **out**?

Following are some more phrasal verbs. Those that have an adverb that can stand in two positions around the object of the phrasal verb are identified by an asterisk (*).

Fill

fill in/out*

1. *mend a hole by adding matter* = The men **filled in** the pothole with asphalt.
2. *write in the blanks of a form* = Put the questionnaire on my desk after you have **filled** it **out**.

fill in for

replace or substitute for someone = Jim is sick, so I have to **fill in for** him today.

fill up*

make full = Go to the gas station and **fill up** the tank.

Give

give away*

1. *relinquish or donate* = The millionaire **gave away** most of his wealth to charity.
2. *reveal private facts about someone or something* = The gangster's girlfriend **gave** him **away**, and he was arrested at his office.

give up*

surrender an object or oneself = I can't **give up** the struggle for humans rights. The soldier raised his hands and **gave up**.

give up on

admit to failure in a relationship or at an activity = I knew you would finish the marathon. I never **gave up on** you.

give in (to)

yield (to someone or something) = I stayed on my diet and didn't **give in to** my craving for chocolate.

give out

wear out or begin to fall apart = That tire is very old and will **give out** before too long.

Go

go for

find someone or something attractive = Bob is so good-looking. I could **go for** him.

go in for

enjoy or *make an activity a favorite* = Jim is athletic and **goes in for** every sport.

go off

1. *explode* = Careful! That bomb could **go off**!
2. *take place or happen* = Her surprise birthday party **went off** just as planned.

go into

1. *explain* = I don't want to **go into** why I'm quitting my job now. Someday I'll tell you.
2. *enter a profession or line of work* = My sister **went into** law.

go over

look carefully at something = I suggest we **go over** the architect's plans one more time.

go through with

complete or carry out a plan to its conclusion = I won't **go through with** it! I won't jump out of this plane!

go out with

date regularly = John has been **going out with** Lisa since March.

EXERCISE 19·3

Write three original sentences with each phrasal verb. In the first sentence, place the adverb in front of the noun object; in the second sentence, place the adverb behind the noun object; and in the third sentence, change the noun object to a pronoun. For example:

(figure out)

I figured out the problem.

I figured the problem out.

I figured it out.

1. (fill in) _____

_____

_____

2. (fill out) _____

_____

_____

3. (fill up) _____

_____

_____

4. (give away) _____

_____

_____

5. (give up) _____

_____

_____

Write an original sentence with each phrasal verb.

1. (fill in for) _____

2. (give up) _____

3. (give up on) _____

4. (give in to) _____

5. (give out) _____

6. (go for) _____

7. (go in for) _____

8. (go into) _____

9. (go through with) _____

10. (go out with) _____

Keep

keep on

continue = **Keep on** reading while I write something on the board.

keep up (with)

1. *prevent someone from sleeping* = We have to **keep** him **up** until the doctor comes.
2. *move at the same pace as someone else* = Slow down! I can't **keep up with** you!

keep out*

stop someone from entering a place = Please **keep** the dog **out.** His feet are dirty.

Let

let down*

1. *lower* = **Let down** the ladder so I can come up into the attic.
2. *disappoint* = I tried to make it here on time. I'm sorry I **let** you **down**.

let in on

share information or a scheme with someone = We're going to make a lot of money, and we're going to **let** you **in on** the deal.

let on

divulge information about someone or something = Don't **let on** to Doris that you know about her illness.

Make

make of

interpret someone or something = What do you **make of** Mary? She starts to cry over nothing.

make out*

see clearly = It's so foggy that I can't **make out** the coastline.

make up*

fabricate or *lie about something* = Why did you **make up** that story about me?

make up with

reconcile = Jack visited his wife last week and **made up with** her.

make up for

compensate for = You can't **make up for** such bad behavior.

Run

run out of

use the last of something = I can't finish the cake. I've **run out of** butter and sugar.

run out on

leave and abandon someone or something = For some reason, Mary **ran out on** her husband and left town.

run over*

1. *step or roll (as in a vehicle) on someone or something* = I think you just **ran over** a plastic bottle.
2. *go beyond a limit* = The president's speech will **run over** an hour.
3. *review or examine something* = We'll be happy to **run over** these documents with you.

run up*

1. *raise something* = They **run** Old Glory **up** every morning at seven.
2. *to incur a debt* = You've **run up** quite a credit card bill.

run up against

encounter an obstacle = We **ran up against** the building commission, and work on the building had to stop.

Rewrite each sentence by changing the position of the adverb in the phrasal verb. Then rewrite the sentence again by changing the noun object to a pronoun. For example:

She figures out the answer.

She figures the answer out.

She figures it out.

1. Try to keep the tourists out a little longer.

   _____

   _____

2. You let down the whole family with your actions.

   _____

   _____

3. It's hard to make the skyline out in this haze.

   _____

   _____

4. Who made up these lies about the mayor?

   _____

   _____

5. You just ran my foot over!

   _____

   _____

6. Let's run up the victory pennant as we come into the harbor.

   _____

   _____

Write an original sentence using the phrasal verb in parentheses.

1. (keep up with) _____

2. (let in on) _____

3. (make of) _____

4. (run up against) _____

5. (keep on) _____

6. (let in on) _____

7. (make up with) _____

8. (run out of) _____

9. (make up for) _____

10. (let on) _____

Set

set against

cause someone to be another person's enemy or adversary = The cunning man **set** his business partners **against** one another.

set off*

cause something to explode = The crew **set off** an explosive to close the opening to the mine.

set off on

begin a journey = My father **set off on** a weekend fishing trip.

set out for

begin a journey with a specific destination = The group **set out for** a two-hour tour of the canyon.

set up*

erect something = Let's **set up** the tents along this stream.

Stand

stand by

give support in a time of difficulty = My parents **stood by** me during that difficult lawsuit.

stand for

1. *be the symbol for something* = The American flag **stands for** liberty and democracy.
2. *tolerate* = My father isn't going to **stand for** any more arguments.

stand in for

be a substitute for someone = When Tim got sick, Laura **stood in for** him.

stand up for

take a defensive position in favor of someone or something = Dr. King **stood up for** civil rights for everyone.

Take

take down*

write something on paper = **Take down** every word the witness says.

take in*

1. *decrease the size of a garment* = It's too loose. **Take** the waist **in** a little.
2. *give someone shelter* = We **took in** a homeless man for a week.
3. *fool or deceive someone* = Somehow they **took** me **in** with that phony scheme.

take off

depart rapidly = When they saw the police, they **took off** down the street.

Turn

turn in(to)*

1. *go to bed* = It's ten o'clock. I think I'll **turn in**.
2. *give someone to the authorities* = Our neighbors **turned** the thief **in**, and he was arrested.
3. *change into a different kind of person or thing* = Your son has **turned into** quite the gentleman.

turn up*

1. *increase the volume or output of something* = It's getting cold. Let's **turn** the heat **up**.
2. *happen to appear* = I hadn't seen my cousin in eight years, and today he suddenly **turned up**.

Walk

walk up to

approach = Tom **walked up to** the clerk and asked where the men's department was.

walk out on

abandon = For some reason, Mr. Barnes **walked out on** his wife and two children.

EXERCISE
19·7

Write three original sentences using each phrasal verb. In the first sentence, place the adverb before of the noun object; in the second sentence, place the adverb after the noun object; and in the third sentence, change the noun object to a pronoun. For example:

(figure out)

We have to figure our taxes out.

We have to figure out our taxes.

We have to figure them out.

1. (set off) _____

_____

_____

2. (set up) _____

_____

_____

3. (take in) _____

_____

_____

4. (take down) _____

_____

_____

5. (turn in) _____

_____

_____

6. (turn up) _____

_____

_____

EXERCISE
19·8

Write original sentences with the phrasal verbs in parentheses.

1. (set against) _____

2. (set out for) _____

3. (stand by) _____

4. (stand for) _____

5. (stand up for) _____

6. (take down) _____

7. (take off) _____

8. (turn in[to]) _____

9. (walk up to) _____

10. (walk out on) _____

It is important to remember that the words that make up a phrasal verb do not always give a clue to the meaning of the phrase. Sometimes even an ordinary verb and a preposition are identical to a phrasal verb. One such example is **come to**.

> **Ordinary verb and preposition: Come to** the window and look at the parade.
>
> **Phrasal verb:** When the man **comes to**, give him some water and let him rest. (*When the man awakens, . . .*)

The point is that care must be taken when using phrasal verbs. Consult a dictionary for accuracy, and remember that *practice makes perfect*.

Writing

·20·

This chapter provides a variety of opportunities to do some creative writing. You will write original sentences in various formats and complete missing lines from dialogues. Do not be afraid to experiment and apply new ideas that you have developed from your experience with the other chapters. Use any resources that will help you to write accurately.

EXERCISE
20·1

Write original sentences using the phrase provided in parentheses as described in each line. For example:

(my brother)

subject of the sentence: *My brother used to work in a factory.*

direct object: *Professor Michaels would like to meet my brother.*

(our new neighbors)

1. subject of the sentence

_____

2. direct object

_____

3. object of the preposition **with**

_____

4. indirect object

_____

5. subject of a future tense passive voice sentence

_____

6. direct object in a subjunctive sentence

_____

7. object of the preposition **for**

_____

8. subject of a past tense passive voice sentence

_____

9. object of the preposition **by** in a passive voice sentence

_____

10. indirect object

_____

_____

Write original sentences using the phrase provided in parentheses as described in each line.

(your daughter)

1. a possessive

_____

2. in a comparison following **than**

_____

3. indirect object

_____

4. object of the preposition **because of**

_____

5. antecedent of the relative pronoun **that**

_____

6. antecedent of the relative pronoun **who**

_____

7. direct object

_____

8. subject of the verb **be supposed to**

_____

9. object of the preposition **by** in a passive voice sentence

_____

10. modified by a past participle

_____

_____

Write original sentences using the phrase provided in parentheses as described in each line.

(a few mistakes)

1. subject

_____

2. in a comparison following **than**

_____

3. direct object

_____

4. object of the preposition **because of**

_____

5. antecedent of the relative pronoun **that**

_____

6. antecedent of the relative pronoun **which**

_____

7. in a subordinating clause beginning with **if**

_____

8. subject of a present perfect tense sentence

_____

9. object of the phrasal verb **go over**

_____

10. modified by a present participle

_____

EXERCISE
20·4

Write original sentences using the phrase provided in parentheses as described in each line.

(one of the students)

1. subject

_____

2. in a comparison following **than**

_____

3. indirect object

_____

4. object of the preposition **from**

_____

5. object in a subordinating clause

_____

6. antecedent of the relative pronoun **whose**

_____

7. direct object

_____

8. subject of the verb **have to**

_____

9. subject of a passive voice sentence

_____

10. modified by a superlative adjective

_____

EXERCISE
20·5

Write original sentences using the phrase provided in parentheses as described in each line.

(this suitcase)

1. object of the preposition **of**

_____

2. in a comparison following **than**

_____

3. object in a restrictive relative clause

_____

4. object of the preposition **into**

_____

5. antecedent of the relative pronoun **which**

_____

6. subject of the verb phrase **would be**

_____

7. direct object

_____

8. subject of the verb phrase **should have**

_____

9. subject of a passive voice sentence in the future tense

_____

10. modified by a present participle

_____

EXERCISE
20·6

Complete each sentence with any appropriate phrase that includes the vocabulary in parentheses. For example:

Tom is sleeping on the floor, but _____.

(sofa) Tom is sleeping on the floor, but _the dog is sleeping on the sofa_.

I found something in the attic that _____.

1. (belong) _____

2. (interesting) _____

3. (hidden) _____

4. (was stolen) _____

If _____, why do you continue to live here?

5. (put up with) _____

6. (impatient) _____

7. (be up to) _____

8. (go out with) _____

Tomorrow we're going to _____.

9. (mountains) _____

10. (rebuild) _____

11. (relatives) _____

12. (fill up) _____

His lawyer said that _____.

13. (should have) _____

14. (must have) _____

15. (accident) _____

16. (a heavy fine) _____

I would have come here sooner _____.

17. (know) _____

18. (get) _____

19. (let in on) _____

20. (be able to) _____

21. (than) _____

The little boy, _____, ran up to his father.

22. (crying) _____

23. (having heard) _____

24. (seeing) _____

25. (having found) _____

EXERCISE
20·7

In the blank provided, write a line of dialogue that fits the conversation. For example:

I'm going downtown.

Are you going by bus or subway?

I prefer to go by bus.

1. My son is finally getting good grades in school.

   _____

   Maybe my son can help her.

2. Are there any good movies playing tonight?

   _____

   They don't sound interesting, but I don't feel like staying home.

3. My parents' anniversary is next Saturday.

Are you planning on getting them a gift?

_____

4. Do you like this green and white tie?

_____

I think bow ties look funny.

5. Where did I put my wallet?

_____

Impossible. I always put it on my dresser.

6. Does your daughter like living in Montreal?

She loves it but is having trouble with the French language.

_____

7. I think you look wonderful in that dress.

_____

Really? I think it's perfect for you.

8. Are you visiting our city for the first time?

Yes, and I don't know what to see first.

_____

9 That looks like an expensive camera.

_____

It must be a digital camera.

10. How much time will you be spending in Miami?

_____

You're very lucky.

11. Is Bob going out with Ashley now?

_____

But I saw Bob with Ashley at the mall.

12. Do you have a new cell number?

_____

That's strange. Whenever I call, I just get your voice mail.

13. Maria likes your brother a lot.

_____

Athletes are always so popular.

14. My cousin went skydiving last week.

_____

They say it's quite safe.

15. This is third time it's rained this week.

_____

But a little warm sunshine would be nice.

_____

EXERCISE
20·8

Complete the lines of dialogue with any appropriate phrases.

1. Ms. Patel: It's good to see you again. _____?

2. Mr. Brooks: No, my wife is still in Europe. _____.

3. Ms. Patel: I didn't know that she speaks Spanish. _____.

4. Mr. Brooks: I'm anxious for her to come home. _____?

5. Ms. Patel: Yes, my son goes to Yale. _____.

6. Mr. Brooks: Next year our boy goes away to school. _____.

7. Ms. Patel: Yes, they grow up so fast. _____.

8. Mr. Brooks: That's true. _____?

9. Ms. Patel: We don't do much traveling anymore. _____.

10. Mr. Brooks: It was nice talking to you. _____.

EXERCISE
20·9

Complete the lines of dialogue with any appropriate phrases.

1. Tom: Is that Mary Larson over there? _____?

2. Bill: No, I think that's her cousin. _____.

3. Tom: He's really tall. _____?

4. Bill: If he does, I want him on my team. _____.

5. Tom: I'm not good at basketball. _____.

6. Bill: That's because you're so fast on your skates. _____.

7. Tom: Look. My sister's going into the drugstore. _____?

8. Bill: Girls are always buying cosmetics. _____.

9. Tom: She's already got a boyfriend. _____.

10. Bill: I'm only two years younger than she is. _____.

EXERCISE
20·10

Complete the lines of dialogue with any appropriate phrases.

1. Uncle Ben: So, you finally came to visit me. _____?

2. Jim: I haven't seen you since July. _____.

3. Uncle Ben: How is life as a college man? _____?

4. Jim: I study a lot. _____.

5. Uncle Ben: Young men need time to relax. _____.

6. Jim: I don't date much. _____.

7. Uncle Ben: Maybe you need to get a part-time job. _____?

8. Jim: I'm thinking about doing that. _____.

9. Uncle Ben: I could lend you my car for a while. _____.

10. Jim: But I couldn't afford the gas. _____.

11. Uncle Ben: Do you have time for some lunch? _____.

12. Jim: That sounds great. _____.

APPENDIX
Homophones

Homophone	Meaning
ad	abbreviated form of *advertisement*
add	find the sum of
aid	assist, help
aide	assistant, helper
ail	be sick
ale	beer
air	what one breathes
heir	one who inherits
aisle	passageway
I'll	contraction of *I will*
isle	island
allowed	past tense of *allow*, permitted
aloud	said in full voice
altar	raised stage for worship
alter	change
ant	insect
aunt	parent's sister
ate	past tense of *eat*
eight	number that follows seven
aural	concerning hearing
oral	of the mouth, spoken
bail	pump water out
bale	bundle hay
bald	hairless
bawled	past tense of *bawl*, cried

Homophone	Meaning
band	company of persons, musical group
banned	not allowed
baron	aristocratic rank
barren	unable to conceive a child
base	bottom support
bass	lowest male singing voice
be	exist
bee	pollinating insect
beach	sandy shoreline
beech	variety of tree
beat	strike
beet	red root plant
beau	boyfriend
bow	fancy knot in a ribbon
bedding	blankets and linens for a bed
betting	placing a bet, gambling
beer	ale
bier	catafalque for a coffin
berry	fruit of a plant
bury	place beneath the earth
berth	where a ship docks
birth	the act of being born
bite	seize with the teeth
byte	eight bits in computing

Homophone	Meaning	Homophone	Meaning
blew	past tense of *blow*	carat	weight measure for gems
blue	azure color	carrot	vegetable
		karat	measure of fineness for gold
bloc	political or military alliance		
block	hinder; square piece of wood	cast	throw, thrust
		caste	artificial class of society
board	plank of wood		
bored	uninterested, indifferent	cede	yield, give up
		seed	ovule for plant reproduction
bold	courageous, daring		
bowled	past tense of *bowl*, knocked down bowling pins	ceiling	overhead covering of a room
		sealing	act of closing tightly
born	brought forth by birth	cell	small room, microscopic protoplasm
borne	past participle of *bear*		
		sell	put up for sale
borough	incorporated village, subdivision		
burrow	dig into the earth	cellar	basement
		seller	person who puts something up for sale
brake	reduce speed		
break	damage, requiring repair	cent	penny
		scent	smell, aroma
bread	basic food made from flour	sent	past tense of *send*
bred	past tense of *breed*		
		cereal	grain
brews	products of brewing, such as ale and beer	serial	successive, arranged in rows
bruise	discolored injury of the skin	chance	fortune, luck
		chants	songs, psalms
bridal	referring to a bride		
bridle	horse's head harness	chased	past tense of *chase*
		chaste	pure
budding	blossoming		
butting	hitting with the head or horns	chews	masticates
		choose	select
but	conjunction meaning *still, yet, however*	chord	harmonic tone
		cord	string, rope
butt	hit with the head or horns	cored	past tense of *core*
buy	purchase	cite	quote
by	near, next to	sight	vision
bye	good-bye, farewell	site	location
cannon	artillery weapon	clause	statement of proviso in a document
canon	criterion, rule of law		
		claws	sharp, curved nails
capital	principal, wealth, seat of government	close	shut
capitol	government building	clothes	raiment, garments

Homophone	Meaning	Homophone	Meaning
coarse	rough	ewe	female sheep
course	path, school program	yew	evergreen tree
		you	second person pronoun
colonel	military officer's rank		
kernel	seed	eye	organ for vision
		I	first person singular pronoun
core	innermost part of a thing		
corps	military unit	faint	become unconscious
		feint	maneuver to confuse
council	official group		an enemy
counsel	adviser		
		fair	just
creak	squeak	fare	money for transportation
creek	brook, stream		
		fairy	imaginary being
crews	plural of *crew*, company	ferry	boat for transporting passengers
	or group of people		or goods
cruise	journey by ship		
		faux	phony, fake
cue	signal, hint word	foe	enemy
queue	line		
		feat	skillful act, achievement
cymbal	gong, percussion instrument	feet	plural of *foot*
symbol	representation		
		find	locate
days	plural of *day*	fined	past tense of *fine*
daze	bewilder, stun		
		fir	pine tree
dear	beloved	fur	animal skin and hair
deer	ruminant mammal		
		flea	wingless insect, parasite
dew	condensation	flee	escape
do	perform		
due	owed	flew	past tense of *fly*
		flu	abbreviation of *influenza*
die	perish, succumb		
dye	color, tint	flour	meal for baking
		flower	a bloom
discussed	talked over		
disgust	sicken	for	on behalf of, on account of
		four	number that follows three
doe	female deer		
dough	moistened flour	foreword	introduction in a book
		forward	in a frontal direction
dual	pertaining to two of		
	a thing	foul	offensive, filthy
duel	combat between two people	fowl	bird
earn	deserve, work for	frees	liberates
urn	large vase	freeze	change into ice

Homophone	Meaning	Homophone	Meaning
gait	stride	heard	past tense of *hear*
gate	door in a fence	herd	animals feeding and traveling together
genes	chromosomes		
jeans	blue jeans	heroin	dangerous narcotic
		heroine	feminine form of *hero*
gnu	South African antelope		
knew	past tense of *know*	higher	comparative of *high*
new	opposite of *old*	hire	employ
gored	past tense of *gore*, pierced	him	objective case of *he*
gourd	melonlike fruit	hymn	religious song
gorilla	ape	hoarse	scratchy sound
guerilla	partisan, underground soldier	horse	equine animal
grate	framework of bars	hoes	plural of *hoe*
great	very large	hose	flexible tube for conveying water
groan	moan	hole	cavity, pit
grown	past participle of *grow*	whole	entire, complete
guessed	past tense of *guess*	hour	sixty minutes
guest	invited person, visitor	our	possessive of *we*
hail	frozen rain	idle	at rest, not working
hale	healthy, hearty	idol	worshipped figure
hair	filaments that grow from the skin, fur	in	preposition meaning *inside of*
hare	rabbit	inn	small hotel
		it's	contraction of *it is*
hall	salon, large room	its	possessive of *it*
haul	pull, transport		
		knead	work into dough
halve	separate into two pieces	need	be in want of, require
have	possess, hold		
		knight	medieval man of arms
hangar	shelter for aircraft	night	darkness after sundown
hanger	object from which something hangs, coat hanger	knot	intertwined rope or cord
		not	negative adverb
hay	dried grasses		
hey	a call, an exclamation	know	have information
		no	negative, opposite of *yes*
he'll	contraction of *he will*		
heal	restore to health	lacks	is in want of or need
heel	back part of the foot	lax	remiss, loose
hear	listen to	ladder	device for climbing
here	located in this place	latter	second of two

Homophone	Meaning	Homophone	Meaning
lain	past participle of *lie*	might	past tense of *may*
lane	narrow path, road	mite	small arachnid
lead	heavy metal	mind	intellect, thoughts
led	past tense of *load*	mined	past tense of *mine*
lean	thin, having little fat	miner	one who digs for ore
lien	legal claim on property	minor	youth, not yet an adult
leased	rented	moan	groan
least	superlative of *little*	mown	past participle of *mow*
lessen	decrease, reduce	moose	large elk
lesson	exercise, learned material	mousse	fluffy dessert
load	burden	morning	time before noon
lode	deposit of valuable mineral	mourning	grieving
loan	something lent	muscle	organ that performs body movements
lone	single, alone	mussel	bivalve mollusk
made	past tense of *make*		
maid	female servant	naval	referring to the navy
		navel	belly button
mail	letters and postcards		
male	referring to men	none	not one
		nun	woman devoted to religion
main	primary		
mane	hair about the necks of animals	oar	paddle for moving a boat
		or	conjunction meaning *either*
maize	corn		
maze	puzzling network of paths	ore	raw mineral
mall	large shopping complex	one	number before two
maul	abuse, manhandle	won	past tense of *win*
manner	mode, method	paced	past tense of *pace*
manor	mansion	paste	glue
marry	wed	packed	past tense of *pack*
merry	happy	pact	agreement, alliance
marshal	police official	pail	bucket
martial	pertaining to the military	pale	ashen, wan
meat	flesh	pain	ache, soreness
meet	encounter	pane	window glass
medal	award	pair	two, a couple
meddle	interfere	pare	cut, shave, peel
metal	substances like iron	pear	sweet fruit

Homophone	Meaning	Homophone	Meaning
passed	past tense of *pass*	quarts	plural of *quart*, quarter of a gallon
past	gone by; before the present	quartz	crystallized silicon
		racket	illegal scheme
patience	calm willingness to wait	racquet	tennis bat
patients	plural of *patient*		
		rain	water from clouds, precipitation
pause	hesitate, linger	reign	rule, be in royal power
paws	plural of *paw*	rein	long belt attached to a harness to guide an animal
peace	opposite of *war*, tranquillity		
piece	part	raise	lift up, elevate
		rays	plural of *ray*, beams of light
peak	mountaintop	raze	tear down, destroy
peek	look furtively		
		rap	knock
peddle	sell a small amount of goods	wrap	cover in paper or material
petal	part of a flower		
		read	past tense of *read*
pi	3.14 in mathematics	red	primary color
pie	pastry filled with fruit		
		read	peruse text
plain	homely, ordinary	reed	thin aquatic plant
plane	flat surface; abbreviated form of *airplane*		
		real	genuine, authentic
		reel	winding device
pleas	plural of *plea*		
please	give pleasure	review	survey or consider again
		revue	theatrical production
plum	purple fruit, fruit tree		
plumb	vertical, perpendicular	right	opposite of *left*; correct
		rite	sacred ritual
pore	perforation in the skin	write	put on paper with pen or pencil
pour	spill in a continuous stream		
		ring	jewelry for a finger
pray	entreat God	wring	twist, squeeze out water
prey	object of a predator		
		road	street
presence	being present, existence	rode	past tense of *ride*
presents	plural of *present*, gifts		
		roe	caviar, fish eggs
principal	first in rank, primary	row	move a boat with oars
principle	rule of conduct, law of nature		
		role	character's part in a play
profit	money earned beyond expenses	roll	move on wheels
prophet	teller of divine messages or the future	root	subterranean part of a plant
		route	highway, itinerary
pudding	flavored dessert	rose	flower
putting	present participle of *put*	rows	plural of *row*

Homophone	Meaning	Homophone	Meaning
rote	mechanical memorization	sole	only, single
wrote	past tense of *write*	soul	immortal essence
rye	grain	some	a few
wry	bent, askew	sum	added total
sacks	bags	son	scion, male offspring
sax	abbreviation of *saxophone*	sun	heavenly body, center of the solar system
sail	travel on water powered by the wind in sails	stair	step
sale	the act of selling, putting up for auction	stare	glare, look intensively
		stake	sharpened wooden post
saver	one who saves	steak	slice of meat
savor	enjoy flavor		
		stationary	fixed, permanent
scene	landscape; place of action in a play	stationery	parchment, writing paper
seen	past participle of *see*	steal	rob, abscond with
		steel	iron
sea	ocean, large body of water		
see	have vision, catch sight of	step	stair
		steppe	broad prairie
seam	edge of two pieces of cloth sewn together	straight	not curved or bent
seem	appear, give an impression	strait	narrow waterway
seaman	sailor	suede	undressed kid leather
semen	male seed	swayed	past tense of *sway*
serf	slave	suite	large hotel room, ensemble
surf	wave breaking on a shoreline	sweet	opposite of *sour*, sugary
sew	fasten with a needle and thread	sundae	ice cream dessert
so	conjunction meaning *in such a way*	Sunday	day that precedes Monday
sow	plant seed	tacks	plural of *tack*
		tax	levy on income or property
side	lateral part of something		
sighed	past tense of *sigh*	tail	hind part of an animal's body
		tale	story
sighs	long sounds of respiration due to fatigue or sadness	taught	past tense of *teach*
size	measurement	taut	tight
slay	kill	tea	herbal drink
sleigh	large sled	tee	small stand for a golf ball
soar	fly and glide	team	group of workers or players
sore	hurt, ache	teem	overflow

Homophone	Meaning	Homophone	Meaning
tear	droplet from the eye	wait	rest patiently, await
tier	row or rank in a series	weight	heaviness
tense	nervous, stressed	war	armed conflict
tents	plural of *tent*	wore	past tense of *wear*
their	possessive of *they*	ware	merchandise, good
there	location in the distance	wear	put on apparel
they're	contraction of *they are*	where	what location
threw	past tense of *throw*	wax	candle paraffin
through	preposition meaning *from end to end*	whacks	plural of *whack*
throne	royal chair	wail	cry
thrown	past participle of *throw*	whale	huge, fishlike mammal
tide	ebb and flow of the sea	we	first person plural pronoun
tied	past tense of *tie*	wee	small
to	toward	we'd	contraction of *we would*
too	also, extremely	weed	wild plant
two	number after one		
		we'll	contraction of *we will*
toe	digit of the foot	wheel	caster, roller
tow	pull		
		we've	contraction of *we have*
troop	military group	weave	work with a loom, produce fabric
troupe	group of performers		
		weak	not strong
use	employ	week	seven days
yews	evergreen trees		
		weather	atmospheric conditions
vain	conceited	whether	conjunction meaning *in case, if*
vane	weathercock		
vein	blood vessel	which	what person or thing
		witch	sorceress, evil woman
vary	alter, diversify		
very	extremely	whine	cry plaintively
		wine	alcoholic beverage from grapes
vice	corruption, wicked habit		
vise	brace, clamp	who's	contraction of *who is*
		whose	belonging to whom
wader	a person who wades or walks through water		
		wood	product from trees
waiter	a server in a restaurant	would	past tense of *will*
waist	part of the body between the chest and hips	you'll	contraction of *you will*
		yule	Christmastime
waste	squander		
		your	possessive of *you*
		you're	contraction of *you are*

Answer key

1 Definite versus indefinite articles

1·1   1. thə   2. thee   3. thee   4. thə   5. thee   6. thə   7. thə   8. thə   9. thə   10. thee   11. thee   12. thə   13. thee   14. thee   15. thə   16. thə   17. thə   18. thee   19. thə   20. thee

1·2   1. the State of Florida   2. The problem; the lack   3. the children; the park   4. the tour guide; the tourists   5. The boys; the girls   6. the guest room   7. The newspaper; the porch; the pouring rain   8. the war   9. The scholarship winner; the East   10. the wall

1·3   1. an   2. an   3. a   4. a   5. a   6. a   7. a   8. a   9. a   10. an   11. an   12. an   13. a   14. a   15. a   16. an   17. an   18. an   19. an   20. an

1·4   1. The; the; a   2. a; the   3. the; the; the   4. a/the; the   5. a; the; a   6. a; the; the   7. a; the; a   8. an; the; a; the; the   9. a; the; the; a/the; a/the   10. a; the; the; the

1·5
1. The boys played in the fields with dogs.
2. We have new gardeners for the new nurseries.
3. When on vacations in Hawaii, I often visit young surfers at the beaches.
4. If you can find rackets, we can go to the tennis courts and try to find partners for you.
5. The children never watch movies of which the nannies do not approve.
6. If I had puppies, I would give the puppies to lonely men or women.
7. The reasons for my tardiness are simple: there were accidents on the snowy roads, and the police officers halted all traffic.
8. Put candles on the tables and bottles of white wine in the coolers, so we can celebrate.
9. Did you send the lawyers telegrams or e-mails?
10. Pretty women approached the cars and held up signs asking for help.

1·6
1. The boy ran across the garden and ruined a row of vegetables.
2. A rainstorm and a windy day made the sightseeing trip miserable.
3. The new student had to carry a tray of milk cartons into a classroom.
4. Is a tourist from a European country a better tipper than a tourist from Asia?
5. The reindeer bolted into the field and startled the resting goose.

1·7   1. b   2. c   3. d   4. c   5. c

2 Capitalization and punctuation

2·1   1. During; I; Mr. Smith   2. Are; Frank; Ellen   3. I; Spotty   4. Why; Professor Keller; Edward; My; John   5. Dr. Parsons   6. Don't; Help   7. The   8. We; Vice President Biden   9. Last; Mary; I; I   10. Could; Mrs. Martin; She's

2·2   1. Mr. President; Iran   2. Please   3. When; Senator Smith   4. She; Windsor Castle   5. Captain Jones; I; Russian; Bering Sea   6. Did; Ms. Keller; Declaration of Independence   7. My; Boston; Philadelphia   8. My; Angelina Jolie; California   9. The; New York University   10. Turn; Mr. Brown; I; I; Europe

2·3   1. My; *The New York Times*   2. Our; *To Kill a Mockingbird*   3. The Department of State
4. *Life*; *Mississippi*   5. Professor Howard's; *The War Against Poverty*   6. The; London; Gainsborough
7. Tony   8. Mark; Helen; *Our Town*   9. I; Ford; Cadillac   10. The; Indians; West

2·4   1. I; German   2. Michelangelo; Renaissance; He, He, And   3. My; Ms. Butterworth   4. We   5. When;
Midwest; Chicago; Michigan Avenue   6. In; *A New Theory*; *Capitalism*; Miriam Thorn; University;
Toronto   7. Although; I; I   8. Most; English; Introduction; Computers   9. The; Westminster Abbey;
Saturday   10. My; *The Wall Street Journal*

2·5   1. p.m.   2. manuscript?   3. 2.5   4. now!   5. work?   6. out! corner!   7. leaves.   8. B.S.   9. be?
10. here! / here.   11. much! / much.   12. class.   13. there?   14. birthday.   15. $15.99

2·6   1. Uncle Tim, a dental surgeon, lives in Oakland on Main Street.
2. Today I want to take a drive out into the country, because the weather is so nice.
3. During my first semester in college, I became interested in biology.
4. I'll send you some postcards when I get to Paris.
5. As the handsome man entered the room, all eyes followed his every move.
6. Oh, you really look wonderful in that dress.
7. Jim, would you help me get the picnic basket, cooler, and blankets from the attic?
8. The boys, as usual, came in from the yard to wash up.
9. Someone asked him, "Are you feeling all right, Mr. Dunn?"
10. Our house is at 2890 Miller Street, Streeterville, Iowa.

2·7   *The following are some sample answers:*
1. The working-class population needs more jobs.
2. He is such a narrow-minded man.
3. He is really much too strong-willed.
4. He was empty-handed when he got home.
5. I love an action-packed film.
6. She was such a soft-spoken lady.
7. It was a one-time opportunity.
8. White-collar workers often get paid more.
9. Her close-up photographs looked beautiful.
10. They are such time-consuming problems.
11. You can make any long-distance call from here.
12. The five-year-old boy played on the living room floor.
13. They lived in a far-off land.
14. She is a blond-haired beauty.
15. Our year-end inventory takes a lot of time.

2·8   1. Their conversation was always one·sided, but Tom didn't complain, because he loved her dearly.
2. I've always wanted a long-term relationship, but I'm worried, because I think you like me because I'm
well-to-do.
3. She'll get you a printout of the article, and you can work on it in my office.
4. Don't you wonder why Ms. Brown said, "I can't believe they're firing me?"
5. "Get your hands off me!" she shouted at her brother-in-law.
6. The twins were born on June 5, 1998, and our six-year-old was born just two years later on the same date.
7. He's been taking Introduction to Computer Science at the University of Chicago since last September.
8. In most of Asia, you'll discover that the people's diet consists mainly of rice, beans, and fish.
9. Professor Simpson was more than a teacher: He was also marvelous speaker. He published several books.
He was even a great ballroom dancer.
10. Oh, no! We'll have to leave for the station by 6:30 a.m. if we want to catch the seven-o'clock train to Boston.

3   Homophones

3·1   1. dear   2. capital   3. scent   4. daze   5. carrots   6. ale   7. heir   8. due   9. bald   10. deer

3·2   *The following are some sample answers:*
1. The general's aide is in the next room.
2. My mother still ails, despite her long treatment.
3. I do what I can to help them.

4. A huge bear came slowly into our camp.
5. The capital of Austria is Vienna.
6. When is the plane due to arrive?
7. She sent me a short letter.
8. In summer she usually has bare shoulders.
9. It's much too cold for me.
10. We spent a few days in Montreal.
11. The dew on the grass glistens.
12. These people need first aid.
13. Your mother is such a dear.
14. I woke up in a daze.
15. That's supposed to be fourteen-karat gold.
16. I think I'm going bald.
17. What is that strange scent?
18. The donkey gnawed on the carrot I held.
19. I don't have a cent left to my name.
20. The baby bawled until his mother showed up.

3·3 *The following are some sample answers:*
1. Perhaps I should buy a metal gate.
2. Yes, please hand me the bag of flour.
3. They're butting their heads against one another.
4. That's a pregnant doe.
5. He always meddles in our affairs.
6. What's the fare to the new mall?
7. Do you always have fresh flowers in your house?
8. Yes, I'm going to earn thirty dollars more a week.
9. I know. It's not fair.
10. I dyed it.
11. What a strange gait that man has.
12. Let's get a ladder and climb up to it.
13. No, we prefer a new house.
14. You're right. I'll get the big urn from the garage.
15. I injured my heel while jogging.
16. I knew Jack when he still lived in Cleveland.
17. No, that's an expensive yew.
18. That's good. Lead pipes can be dangerous.
19. I thought we discussed all this last night.
20. Well, the dough is finally ready.

3·4 *The following are some sample answers:*
1. They sent their son to a naval academy.
   Why are you tickling your navel?
2. They had four candy bars and gave me none.
   My sister wants to be a nun.
3. Did you drop the oar in the water?
   I want to be an astronaut or a firefighter.
   They bring tons of ore out of the mine each day.
4. I peddle old books at the flea market.
   The roses are dying. Their petals are falling on the table.
   Put your foot on the brake pedal. You're going too fast.
5. I love chocolate pudding.
   She's putting her running shoes on now.
6. We need two quarts of milk.
   Is that lens made of quartz?
7. They're trying to raise the sunken boat.
   Dim rays of light broke through the window.
   The old church was dangerous and had to be razed.
8. Someone was rapping quietly at the door.
   I'll wrap the gift in some pretty paper.

9. I only memorized the poem by rote.
    Susan wrote them a long letter.
10. My brother wanted to learn to sew.
    She plays the harp so beautifully.
    The whole family sows the garden every spring.
11. Their house is on Hill Street.
    Do you know the man over there?
    They're going to be guests at our house tonight.
12. The soldier threw his body over the grenade.
    We cautiously walked through the dark tunnel.
13. I don't like to wait so long to see the doctor.
    The weight of this box is too much for me.
14. Get more wood for the fireplace.
    Would you care to dance with me?
15. Your sister is really a smart girl.
    You're in the army now, so act like a soldier.

4 Verb oddities

4·1
1. That girl's my sister.
    That girl's not my sister.
    That girl isn't my sister.
    Isn't that girl my sister?
2. We're tired.
    We're not tired.
    We aren't tired.
    Aren't we tired?
3. You're a good friend.
    You're not a good friend.
    You aren't a good friend.
    Aren't you a good friend?
4. They're at home.
    They're not at home.
    They aren't at home.
    Aren't they at home?
5. He's strong.
    He's not strong.
    He isn't strong.
    Isn't he strong?

4·2
1. They do not spend the summer in Canada.
    They don't spend the summer in Canada.
    Do they spend the summer in Canada?
    Don't they spend the summer in Canada?
2. That man does not have her wallet.
    That man doesn't have her wallet.
    Does that man have her wallet?
    Doesn't that man have her wallet?
3. She does not do me a favor.
    She doesn't do me a favor.
    Does she do me a favor?
    Doesn't she do me a favor?
4. They do not buy a new SUV.
    They don't buy a new SUV.
    Do they buy a new SUV?
    Don't they buy a new SUV?
5. Jessica does not go to college.
    Jessica doesn't go to college.
    Does Jessica go to college?
    Doesn't Jessica go to college?

6. We do not ski every winter.
   We don't ski every winter.
   Do we ski every winter?
   Don't we ski every winter?

4·3
1. Past: She brought home a friend.
   Present perfect: She has brought home a friend.
   Future: She will bring home a friend.
   Question: Will she bring home a friend?
2. Past: The boys ate all the cake.
   Present perfect: The boys have eaten all the cake.
   Future: The boys will eat all the cake.
   Question: Will the boys eat all the cake?
3. Past: I cut some bread for sandwiches.
   Present perfect: I have cut some bread for sandwiches.
   Future: I will cut some bread for sandwiches.
   Question: Shall I cut some bread for sandwiches?
4. Past: You weren't a good musician.
   Present perfect: You haven't been a good musician.
   Future: You won't be a good musician.
   Question: Won't you be a good musician?
5. Past: The women sewed a quilt.
   Present perfect: The women have sewed/sewn a quilt.
   Future: The women will sew a quilt.
   Question: Will the women sew a quilt?
6. Past: Jim didn't have enough change.
   Present perfect: Jim hasn't had enough change.
   Future: Jim won't have enough change.
   Question: Won't Jim have enough change?
7. Past: That rude question cost him his job.
   Present perfect: That rude question has cost him his job.
   Future: That rude question will cost him his job.
   Question: Will that rude question cost him his job?
8. Past: Mark and Joe didn't have enough time.
   Present perfect: Mark and Joe haven't had enough time.
   Future: Mark and Joe won't have enough time.
   Question: Won't Mark and Joe have enough time?
9. Past: We met at four o'clock.
   Present perfect: We have met at four o'clock.
   Future: We shall/will meet at four o'clock.
   Question: Shall we meet at four o'clock?
10. Past: Laura speeded/sped down the street.
    Present perfect: Laura has speeded/sped down the street.
    Future: Laura will speed down the street.
    Question: Will Laura speed down the street?
11. Past: I let you try it on your own.
    Present perfect: I have let you try it on your own.
    Future: I will let you try it on your own.
    Question: Shall I let you try it on your own?
12. Past: Jim went to night school.
    Present perfect: Jim has gone to night school.
    Future: Jim will go to night school.
    Question: Will Jim go to night school?
13. Past: Tim saw a great movie.
    Present perfect: Tim has seen a great movie.
    Future: Tim will see a great movie.
    Question: Will Tim see a great movie?

14. Past: The girls did a project together.
    Present perfect: The girls have done a project together.
    Future: The girls will do a project together.
    Question: Will the girls do a project together?
15. Past: I was your mentor.
    Present perfect: I have been your mentor.
    Future: I shall/will be your mentor.
    Question: Shall I be your mentor?

4·4
1. Past: She was cutting out interesting articles.
    Present perfect: She has been cutting out interesting articles.
    Future: She will be cutting out interesting articles.
2. Past: I was having terrible headaches.
    Present perfect: I have been having terrible headaches.
    Future: I shall/will be having terrible headaches.
3. Past: James was learning to play the flute.
    Present perfect: James has been learning to play the flute.
    Future: James will be learning to play the flute.
4. Past: Mr. Gardner was teaching that class.
    Present perfect: Mr. Gardner has been teaching that class.
    Future: Mr. Gardner will be teaching that class.
5. Past: The moon was shining over the lake.
    Present perfect: The moon has been shining over the lake.
    Future: The moon will be shining over the lake.
6. Past: Why was that man beating his horse?
    Present perfect: Why has that man been beating his horse?
    Future: Why will that man be beating his horse?
7. Past: We were skiing in the Alps.
    Present perfect: We have been skiing in the Alps.
    Future: We shall/will be skiing in the Alps.
8. Past: My brothers were going on vacation together.
    Present perfect: My brothers have been going on vacation together.
    Future: My brothers will be going on vacation together.
9. Past: You were being rude.
    Present perfect: —
    Future: —
10. Past: They were buying a house in the suburbs.
    Present perfect: They have been buying a house in the suburbs.
    Future: They will be buying a house in the suburbs.

5   Tense usage

5·1
1. The children are learning about bears.
2. She is writing a letter to her senator.
3. Is your aunt living in a retirement home?
4. I am being very polite to him.
5. The dogs are lying in a corner and sleeping.
6. Tom is having a party.
7. Are you being funny?
8. The fraternity brothers are building a bonfire.
9. Eric is listening to a new rap artist.
10. Are you speaking Arabic?
11. Sophia is spending a lot of time with her grandmother.
12. They are earning money for a vacation.
13. The little boy is being naughty.
14. It is getting cold again.
15. The roses are dying.

5·2 *The following are some sample answers:*
1. it started to rain
2. I came out of my tent
3. the blizzard began
4. Mom called from the kitchen
5. their coach blew the whistle
6. everyone was waiting for the turkey to arrive
7. I was reading the newspaper
8. the man was running from the burning house
9. We were just sitting down at the table
10. her students were lining up for recess

5·3 *The following are some sample answers:*
1. we were coming in for a landing
2. John was walking along the edge of the pool
3. I was studying German
4. the painters were painting the second floor.
5. we were standing in front of the buffet
6. he was learning English
7. you're earning a good salary
8. the construction crew is working so hard
9. he is walking by himself
10. you are learning new skills

5·4
1. Past: I was learning to speak Japanese.
   Present perfect: I have been learning to speak Japanese.
   Past perfect: I had been learning to speak Japanese.
2. Past: They sang at the top of their voices.
   Present perfect: They have sung at the top of their voices.
   Past perfect: They had sung at the top of their voices.
3. Past: Some boys marched alongside the soldiers.
   Present perfect: Some boys have marched alongside the soldiers.
   Past perfect: Some boys had marched alongside the soldiers.
4. Past: We were preparing a special dinner.
   Present perfect: We have been preparing a special dinner.
   Past perfect: We had been preparing a special dinner.
5. Past: Was Martin going to college?
   Present perfect: Has Martin been going to college?
   Past perfect: Had Martin been going to college?

5·5
1. Future: Jack will describe what he saw.
   Future perfect: Jack will have described what he saw.
2. Future: No one will be rude.
   Future perfect: No one will have been rude.
3. Future: Will you be reading his latest novel?
   Future perfect: Will you have been reading his latest novel?
4. Future: The girls will look everywhere for the cat.
   Future perfect: The girls will have looked everywhere for the cat.
5. Future: Professor Jones will be speaking for a long time.
   Future perfect: Professor Jones will have been speaking for a long time.

5·6 *The following are some sample answers:*
1. to help you with your homework
2. I am going
3. to make a doctor's appointment yesterday
4. We were going
5. to spend the night at your house

5·7
1. Mary frequently wrote a letter to her brother.
2. I will usually wear a dark blue suit.
3. John and Laura have never lived in a tiny apartment.
4. The surgeon scrubs his hands several times a day.
5. He had seldom played tennis with his boss.

6. We sometimes argued about our bills.
7. Ms. Garcia tends to her garden once a week.
8. Does the lawyer often appear in court?
9. My relatives have tried to get a visa many times.
10. They always brought the children gifts.

6   Passive versus static passive

6·1
1. The puppies have been sold by my sister.
   The puppies have been sold.
2. Three houses were badly damaged by the storm.
   Three houses were badly damaged.
3. A book on the subject of art history will be written by Ms. Patel.
   A book on the subject of art history will be written.
4. The town hall had been destroyed by a terrible fire.
   The town hall had been destroyed.
5. The horses are trained for the rodeo by my brother.
   The horses are trained for the rodeo.
6. The drunken man was slapped across the face by Jim.
   The drunken man was slapped across the face.
7. Nearly a hundred planes were transported across the Atlantic by the aircraft carrier.
   Nearly a hundred planes were transported across the Atlantic.
8. A poem about springtime will be written by her.
   A poem about springtime will be written.
9. The pickpocket has been captured and arrested by the police.
   The pickpocket has been captured and arrested.
10. Our new car was crushed by a fallen tree.
    Our new car was crushed.

6·2
1. The puppies were being sold by my sister.
   The puppies were being sold.
2. Three houses were being damaged by the storm.
   Three houses were being damaged.
3. A book on the subject of art history is being written by Ms. Patel.
   A book on the subject of art history is being written.
4. The town hall is being destroyed by a terrible fire.
   The town hall is being destroyed.
5. The horses are being trained for the rodeo by my brother.
   The horses are being trained for the rodeo.
6. The drunken man was being slapped across the face by Jim.
   The drunken man was being slapped across the face.
7. Nearly a hundred planes were being transported across the Atlantic by the aircraft carrier.
   Nearly a hundred planes were being transported across the Atlantic.
8. A poem about springtime is being written by her.
   A poem about springtime is being written.
9. The pickpockets were being captured and arrested by the police.
   The pickpockets were being captured and arrested.
10. Our new car is being crushed by a fallen tree.
    Our new car is being crushed.

6·3
The following are some sample answers:
1. The children must be found as soon as possible.
2. The old TV is not able to be repaired anymore.
3. She has to be driven to the airport by John.
4. Should the woman be questioned about it again?
5. Maria wants to be invited to the prom.
6. The hero is supposed to be rewarded with a medal.
7. This message needs to be sent immediately.
8. The money may be transferred to your bank today.
9. The car might be sold at auction.
10. The crystal vase can be broken quite easily.

1. The girls are bought some ice cream by Martin.
   Some ice cream is bought for the girls by Martin.
2. My neighbors are being lent valuable tools by me.
   Valuable tools are being lent to my neighbors by me.
3. She has been written a long letter by Jack.
   A long letter has been written to her by Jack.
4. Mr. Jordan will be given this gift by Ms. Patel.
   This gift will be given to Mr. Jordan by Ms. Patel.
5. I was found a nice apartment in Brooklyn by the realtor.
   A nice apartment in Brooklyn was found for me by the realtor.
6. The horse is fed oats by the farmer.
   Oats are being fed to the horse by the farmer.
7. The hero is being presented (with) a medal by the mayor.
   A medal is being presented to the hero by the mayor.
8. She was brought some chocolates by the handsome man.
   Some chocolates were brought to her by the handsome man.
9. He was being sent little gifts by her.
   Little gifts were being sent to him by her.
10. The homeless man will be given a place to live by someone.
    A place to live will be given to the homeless man by someone.

6·5 *The following are some sample answers:*

1. The houses are being painted by a large crew of men.
   The houses are painted.
2. Several windows are being broken by the hailstorm.
   Several windows are broken.
3. The tabletop is being scratched by the sharp toy.
   The tabletop is scratched.
4. The iron bar is being bent by that large machine.
   The iron bar is bent.
5. The furniture is being sold at an auction.
   The furniture is sold.

7 Subject-verb agreement

7·1 1. am   2. have   3. Does   4. are   5. appears   6. have   7. is   8. wants   9. plays   10. write

7·2 *The following are some sample answers:*

1. receives a prize
2. is going to earn top marks
3. is flawed
4. is of a different size
5. understands calculus
6. is a good choice for my needs
7. is delicious
8. makes a beautiful sound of its own
9. is going to be selected for the play
10. has the right to run for office

7·3 *The following are some sample answers:*

1. spend a lot of time watching TV
2. are chosen for the team
3. is strong enough
4. Is; spent on Facebook
5. who use this service is well over a million
6. are quite friendly
7. has a son or daughter serving in the military
8. is melting
9. Does; need more time to finish
10. are simply false

7·4 *The following are some sample answers:*
1. is the amount of time he'll spend in jail
2. has to find a solution to this problem
3. cut more evenly
4. spends a lot of money to help the poor
5. Are; in the medicine cabinet
6. come together to help plant a garden
7. need to be ironed
8. is my favorite class
9. is opening its doors on July 10
10. is an important commodity

8 Verbs and prepositions

8·1 1. in 2. in/into 3. to 4. on 5. to 6. between/next to/near 7. to 8. to 9. about/with
10. to 11. next to/near 12. to 13. about/of 14. on 15. into

8·2 1. know 2. speak/talk 3. spoke/talked 4. go/drive/fly/travel 5. talks/speaks/writes
6. send/write 7. say/report 8. read/wrote 9. knows/speaks/tells/talks/reads/writes 10. ask

8·3 1. stands; for 2. laughed; at 3. look; into 4. settled; into 5. care; for 6. staring; at 7. waited;
for 8. asked; for 9. put/place/lay; on 10. shouting; at/calling; to 11. cares; for 12. climb; up
13. cry; over 14. read; for/to 15. come; between 16. fell; into 17. shout; at 18. speak/talk/read/
write; about/of 19. stand; for 20. writes; for

9 Subjunctive

9·1 1. The angry woman demanded that someone pay for the accident.
2. The angry woman demanded that we be better behaved the next time.
3. The angry woman demanded that the child use no more naughty words.
4. The angry woman demanded that I be more helpful in the future.
5. The angry woman demanded that the pickpocket return her purse immediately.
6. I really prefer you speak to me in English or Italian.
7. I really prefer your brother be a bit more polite.
8. I really prefer Ms. Patel learn a different poem by heart.
9. I really prefer the tourists be ready to depart at noon.
10. I really prefer it never happen again.

9·2 *The following are some sample answers:*
1. the student be quieter
2. Mary put on a warmer coat
3. her son come home safely
4. the soldier prepare the gun
5. she bc in the play too
6. Mr. Hardy be fired
7. no one be alone in the pool at any time
8. John leave so soon
9. the airplane take off in 10 minutes
10. Tim rewrite his essay
11. everyone remain calm
12. Laura have time to think about it
13. your group depart a bit later
14. she forget about him altogether
15. the team practice more often

9·3 1. If only the weather stayed warm.
2. If only I had not broken that window.
3. If only we were better friends now.
4. If only she had learned about it from her daughter.
5. If only no one had heard what I said.
6. If only you had not been right about it.

7. If only I had seen that car coming.
8. If only the Cubs won the pennant.
9. If only Barbara were still my girlfriend.
10. If only I had a million dollars.

9·4 *The following are some sample answers:*
1. you understood what he said
2. he had no manners at all
3. I were his enemy
4. his voice were good
5. she had no brains

9·5 *The following are some sample answers:*
1. I would be very grateful
2. you would find all the tools you need
3. I would build him a tree house
4. I would miss my ride home
5. he would not be so angry with me
6. I had a nice car
7. they saw me in this old suit
8. the music were better
9. the rain would stop
10. my grandmother came for a visit

9·6 *The following are some sample answers:*
1. she wouldn't have dropped the plates
2. if I had known how beautiful it is
3. John had turned off the TV
4. his father helped him
5. Jim would have been so proud
6. what would you wish for
7. she studied hard
8. we didn't complain
9. Mary would have bought a new dress
10. They would be so thankful
11. he wouldn't have been ill
12. I had been warned about the storm
13. the boys had not made so much noise
14. you would paint it a different color
15. I had asked you out on a date

10 Little versus *few*

10·1 1. Few 2. few 3. little 4. few 5. little 6. Few 7. little 8. Little 9. few 10. little

10·2 1. a little 2. a few 3. A few 4. A little 5. a little 6. a little 7. a few; a few 8. A little 9. a few 10. A little; a few

10·3 *The following are some sample answers:*
1. She had little faith in me.
2. There are few people I trust more than you.
3. We need a little luck.
4. Can we have a few minutes of your time?
5. I got little help from my sons.
6. Few people knew how sick the mayor was.
7. I had to spend a little more time on the project.
8. The trip took a few less hours than expected.

10·4 1. fewer 2. less 3. less 4. fewer 5. Fewer 6. less 7. fewer 8. less 9. fewer 10. less

10·5 *The following are some sample answers:*
1. We talk less than we used to.
2. I have fewer hours to rest now that I'm in my new job.

3. Six days is less time than I need.
4. This plane carries less cargo than the older model.
5. A month was less time than I wanted to spend in the mountains.
6. He needs less courage and more intelligence.
7. Today we have fewer needs than we had in the past.
8. John wants less aggravation from his children.
9. We know fewer people here than we did back home.
10. Fifty cents is less than I need for bus fare.

11 Comparatives and superlatives

11·1   1. wiser; more wisely   2. more stately; —   3. hungrier; more hungrily   4. fatter; —   5. taller; —
6. tenser; more tensely   7. older; —   8. younger; —   9. bolder; more boldly   10. angrier; more angrily
11. gentler; more gently   12. fainter; more faintly   13. stronger; more strongly   14. weaker; more weakly
15. faster; —

11·2   1. more boring; more boringly   2. more flexible; more flexibly   3. busier; more busily   4. smarter; more
smartly   5. more different; more differently   6. more confident; more confidently   7. more intelligent;
more intelligently   8. more accurate; more accurately   9. more hilarious; more hilariously   10. more
sincere; more sincerely   11. more careless; more carelessly   12. more regretful; more regretfully
13. wiser; more wisely   14. stranger; more strangely   15. more reluctant; more reluctantly

11·3   1. large   2. better   3. farther   4. likable   5. bad   6. well/better   7. more   8. less
9. more ridiculous   10. worse

11·4   *The following are some sample answers:*
1. Your manners are worse than ever.
2. These trains travel the most rapidly.
3. They live in the tiniest village in the Alps.
4. They say that Mr. Collins is the richest man around here.
5. I'm not as young as I used to be.
6. The newest model is also the most expensive.
7. Those are the most fragrant roses in the garden.
8. Your cake is more delicious than my pie.
9. Jim's apartment is less cozy than ours.
10. Music is my least difficult subject.
11. I have a simple solution to the problem.
12. The oldest coins are kept in a safe.
13. This is the best coffee I've ever had.
14. The inn is a little farther up the road.
15. The soprano sang most beautifully.
16. That toad is much uglier than the frog.
17. Today is the warmest day of the year.
18. Last week we had the coldest temperature of the winter.
19. The Joneses are the least wealthy family in our town.
20. She moved the most quickly in an emergency.

12 Pronoun varieties

12·1   *The following are some sample answers:*
1. I used to live in Germany.
   My uncle saw me at the mall.
   Laura doesn't want to dance with me.
2. I have always liked you.
   Was this card from you?
   Tom sent you a letter from Boston.
3. He threw the ball to her.
   Did you buy her another gift?
   Her father is the mayor.

4. Someone gave us tickets for the play.
   Our house is on Schiller Lane.
   Ours is the large, white house.
5. Their final exam is on Tuesday.
   Theirs will probably be very difficult.
   They injured themselves in the accident.

12·2   *The following are some sample answers:*
1. I bought myself a new robe.
2. You need to behave yourself.
3. Did she enjoy herself at the party?
4. It buried itself in the sand.
5. We are trying to adjust ourselves to this new life.
6. Why do you pity yourselves?
7. They forgot themselves and danced wildly.
8. My sister stuck herself with a needle.
9. One should control oneself in public.
10. Our neighbors never restrain themselves in an argument.

12·3   1. They   2. it   3. her   4. Her   5. them   6. She   7. him   8. hers   9. them   10. them; him

12·4   1. his   2. theirs   3. Its   4. ours   5. yours   6. mine   7. hers; mine   8. theirs   9. ours   10. yours

12·5   *The following are some sample answers:*
1. Yours was under the bed.
   Yours are a lot nicer than mine.
2. His is brand-new.
   His come from Asia.
3. Hers needs to be repaired.
   Hers cost more than $50.
4. Ours looks very nice.
   Ours were lost in the fire.
5. Theirs must be cared for better.
   Theirs are being polished.

12·6   *The following are some sample answers:*
1. was playing with a toy
2. ever plays with other dogs
3. The men send; many e-mails
4. can you trust
5. is my favorite one
6. are now missing
7. is for John and you
8. made any sense
9. The young lovers buy; little gifts
10. is stored in the warehouse

12·7   *The following are some sample answers*
1. cost a bit less
2. have made a home in our garden
3. passed the exam
4. was just wasted time
5. was delivered on Monday
6. goes right up the chimney
7. none believed me
8. is left over for the boys
9. pout and act like children
10. even stand up and whistle

13 Determiners and adverbs of degree

13·1 *The following are some sample answers:* 1. important 2. elegant 3. lace 4. warmer 5. foreign
6. pretty 7. similar 8. strange 9. red 10. leather

13·2 *The following are some sample answers:*
1. I recently met his lovely wife.
2. There's no fresh water at our campsite.
3. Their unruly children are the plague of our neighborhood.
4. She needs six large eggs for the cakes.
5. Did he have any useful information for you?
6. We spent a great deal of precious time on his silly plan.
7. There is little tasty food in that awful restaurant.
8. Many weary soldiers slept on the ground.
9. Her recent cold made her voice raspy.
10. Few people ever meet the president.
11. A few strong boys were able to pull the old fence down.
12. Many a handsome man asked Jane for her hand in marriage.
13. Each wise man was rewarded by the king.
14. Do you have a lot of difficult homework to do?
15. Thirty elderly citizens demanded a meeting with the mayor.

13·3 *The following are some sample answers:*
1. I've never been to such a great party before.
2. Both my parents are deceased.
3. There is still a lot of work to be done.
4. They have no more patience with the man.
5. Many a day was spent repairing the damage.
6. Why does Father have so little time for me?
7. Maria knew all the answers.
8. He still had a few questions to ask.
9. The few lines of text I read sounded wonderful.
10. The girls need a little encouragement.

13·4 1. b 2. a 3. a 4. d 5. c 6. a 7. b 8. c 9. a 10. d

13·5 *The following are some sample answers:*
1. That piece of rope is not very long.
2. Is he tall enough to play basketball?
3. She has a rather unusual voice.
4. Her answer to my question was somewhat vague.
5. I almost forgot to lock the door.
6. Ms. Johnson is an extremely intelligent lawyer.
7. We had almost finished painting the garage when the storm came up.
8. Aunt Helen just arrived this evening.
9. That lazy dog is kind of old.
10. I'm hardly ready for this exam.
11. The trunk is too heavy to lift.
12. The runners were completely exhausted after the marathon.
13. She was nearly injured in a fall.
14. The rescued swimmer was scarcely alive.
15. The end of his story was sort of sad.

14 Gerunds, infinitives, and participles

14·1 *The following are some sample answers:*
1. The constant bullying
2. jogging
3. Their teacher's singing
4. swimming and working out
5. a good scolding
6. eating junk food

7. Losing to such a weak team
8. that groaning
9. Lying about your debts
10. using some bad language

14·2 *The following are some sample answers:*
1. Always bickering about money drove them to divorce.
2. I thought about returning the books to the library
3. She wasn't amused by Jim's breaking the vase.
4. Drinking and eating too much can ruin your health.
5. Her smiling didn't dissipate her husband's anger.

14·3 *The following are some sample answers:*
1. Hoping to have a home of his own was Tom's dream.
   The catcher, hoping to tag the runner before he ran home, stumbled and fell in the dust.
2. I often think about finding a treasure.
   The judge, rarely finding any free time, fell asleep in his chair.
3. Learning a trade is important.
   Their son, rarely learning anything in school, has failed again.
4. She is known for helping the poor.
   The young man, often helping his neighbor with her chores, has a kind heart.
5. Attending a good college can provide for a solid future.
   The two sisters, seldom attending their classes, spent their time at the mall.

14·4 *The following are some sample answers:*
1. To marry Jack because he's rich
2. To travel by bus
3. to speak some French
4. to love me
5. To be honest with me

14·5
1. I love to read out in the yard.
   I love reading out in the yard.
2. The children were learning to play chess.
   No gerund sentence possible.
3. She continued to drive for several more miles.
   She continued driving for several more miles.
4. Did you remember to pay the water bill?
   Did you remember paying the water bill?
5. Laura liked to swim in a heated pool.
   Laura liked swimming in a heated pool.

14·6 *The following are some sample answers:*
1. To have been fined for speeding hurt his wallet.
2. To have lived in America for so long made him feel like a real American.
3. To have achieved great success hasn't brought Martin much happiness.
4. To have been selected to head the committee wasn't what Laura wanted.
5. To be fired by the new manager came as no surprise.

14·7 *The following are some sample answers:*
1. The returning soldiers marched proudly into town.
   The soldiers, returning to their tents, waited eagerly for some rest.
   The returned copy of the book is not the one I gave you.
   The books, always returned on time, were still in good condition.
2. Father gave him a punishing look.
   Mr. James was a lenient man, never punishing his sons for their sins.
   The punished boy couldn't sit for two days.
   The thief, finally punished for his many crimes, spent 15 years in prison.
3. The recruiting officer just smiled at the young man.
   Sergeant Collins, recruiting men for the army, described life in the military.
   Do you know all the recruited men?
   Three privates, recently recruited for service, were sent to Fort Benning.

4. The following piece of music was composed by one of our students.
   A waltz, following three rigorous polkas, gave everyone a little breather.
   The followed woman was now in a panic.
   This prayer, often followed by a rousing hymn, is one of my favorites.
5. An insulting picture of her was put in the newspaper.
   His brother-in-law, sometimes insulting Mark's intelligence, tries to act important.
   The insulted noble fought a duel.
   The elderly woman, insulted by the man's sarcasm, turned and left the room.

15 Auxiliaries

15·1
1. Present perfect: John has been at work.
   Past perfect: John had been at work.
   Future: John will be at work.
2. Present perfect: Have I visited you often?
   Past perfect: Had I visited you often?
   Future: Shall I visit you often?
3. Present perfect: He has been speaking for two hours.
   Past perfect: He had been speaking for two hours.
   Future: He will be speaking for two hours.
   Future perfect: He will have been speaking for two hours.
4. Present perfect: The little boy has broken the vase.
   Past perfect: The little boy had broken the vase.
   Future: The little boy will break the vase.
   Future perfect: The little boy will have broken the vase.
5. Present perfect: Has she helped out in the kitchen?
   Past perfect: Had she helped out in the kitchen?
   Future: Will she help out in the kitchen?

15·2
1. would   2. Should   3. should have/would have   4. should/would   5. would have   6. should have/would have   7. would have   8. should have   9. Should   10. would have   11. should   12. should have   13. should have/would have   14. would have   15. should have

15·3
1. My daughter could/was able to learn a funny poem.
   My daughter was supposed to learn a funny poem.
   My daughter had to learn a funny poem.
2. Will you have to be home for supper?
   Will you be able to be home for supper?
   Are you going to be home for supper?
3. Someone ought to help the man with his luggage.
   Someone needs to help the man with his luggage.
   Someone has got to help the man with his luggage.
4. Jack must/has to train for the marathon.
   Jack is able to train for the marathon.
   Jack is supposed to train for the marathon.
5. The officer might stamp my passport.
   The officer was supposed to stamp my passport.
   The officer could/was able to stamp my passport.

15·4
1. Past: Ms. Gupta needed to get some sleep.
   Present perfect: Ms. Gupta has needed to get some sleep.
   Future: Ms. Gupta will need to get some sleep.
2. Present: No one can help the poor man.
   Present perfect: No one has been able to help the poor man.
   Future: No one will be able to help the poor man.
3. Present: Jim must/has to be hospitalized.
   Past: Jim had to be hospitalized.
   Future: Jim will have to be hospitalized.
4. Present: Martin can/is not able to go with you.
   Past: Martin could/was not able to go with you.
   Present perfect: Martin has not been able to go with you.

5. Past: He had to take the train to Seattle.
   Present perfect: He has had to take the train to Seattle.
   Future: He will have to take the train to Seattle.

15·5 *The following are some sample answers:*
   1. left the keys in the car
   2. already heard about the accident
   3. met John in London
   4. taken better care of yourself
   5. paid for everyone's dinner last night
   6. used language like that
   7. Ashley must have
   8. I may have
   9. You ought to have
   10. Tom might have

16 Using *get*

16·1
   1. Past: How did you get over that river?
      Present perfect: How have you gotten over that river?
      Future: How will you get over that river?
   2. Present: The weather gets very chilly again.
      Present perfect: The weather has gotten very chilly again.
      Future: The weather will get very chilly again.
   3. Present: She isn't getting all her pay.
      Past: She wasn't getting all her pay.
      Future: She won't be getting all her pay.
   4. Present: We get high marks for our science project.
      Past: We got high marks for our science project.
      Present perfect: We have gotten high marks for our science project.

16·2 *The following are some sample answers:*
   1. Martin got a new suit made.
      We need to get the radio repaired.
   2. I'll get you to your meeting on time.
      Did you get Uncle John to the airport?
   3. He doesn't get my sense of humor.
      I didn't get anything the professor said.
   4. Go get me a cup of coffee, please.
      Can you get me some aspirin at the store?
   5. This is the first time I've ever gotten to hear a concert live.
      As a child, I never got to go to the circus.
   6. I got the last bus to Cleveland.
      Where can I get a taxi?
   7. Laura has been getting gifts from Bob.
      Tom got a slap across the face.
   8. The baby is getting so big.
      Why do you always get angry with me?
   9. We got home in time for dinner.
      They should get to the border before dawn.
   10. You will get a scholarship with those good grades.
      I only get $9 an hour.

16·3
   1. The car is getting repaired by a new mechanic.
   2. Did he get promoted by Mr. Jackson?
   3. You will get rewarded for your service to the community.
   4. Ashley gets kissed by Jim.
   5. I have often gotten massaged for my sore back.
   6. Does Mom like to get pampered on Mother's Day?
   7. She never wanted to get elected governor.
   8. The team will get trained by Coach Henderson.

9. Was the dog getting maltreated?
10. Many citizens were getting robbed in that neighborhood.

16·4   *The following are some sample answers:*
1. A large house is getting built next to ours.
2. The chickens get fed by old Mr. Brown.
3. The garage has gotten painted three times in two years.
4. The blimp was getting inflated by the grounds crew.
5. Tommy never gets driven to school.

16·5   1. a   2. b   3. d   4. d   5. a   6. a   7. a   8. c   9. b   10. b

17 Restrictive and nonrestrictive relative clauses

17·1   1. The boy, who is one of my students, is looking for his dog.
2. Mr. Simmons, who has two daughters, moved here from Canada.
3. The woman, to whom Bob sent several e-mails, is learning Spanish.
4. This room, whose dimensions/the dimensions of which are 15 × 20 feet, will serve as our family room.
5. The new airport, which has three terminals, is located outside of town.
6. The head of the school, whom we recently visited, became quite ill.
7. Jack, whose parents are neighbors of mine, is a student at Harvard.
8. Their children, for whom Tom bought computer games, rarely argue.
9. Professor Hall, with whom Jenny spoke yesterday, is getting on in years.
10. The bed, on which their baby slept comfortably, is brand-new.

17·2   1. The film which is playing right now is very suspenseful.
2. His children who live in Chicago reside on the same street.
3. The teacher whom I saw in the park is Ms. Garcia.
4. Is the woman who bought your house from Ireland?
5. The flowers which I bought for Jane are already wilting.

17·3   *The following are some sample answers:*
1. The building that is located on the corner is a firehouse.
2. The man that I met in the lobby is a chef.
   The man I met in the lobby is a chef.
3. The girl that I gave the book to is learning English.
   The girl I gave the book to is learning English.
4. His uncle that he likes to talk about is 70 years old.
   His uncle he likes to talk about is 70 years old.
5. These are the animals that belong to the circus.
6. The girl that I kissed is over there.
   The girl I kissed is over there.
7. The boys that I bought the ball for are all under 10.
   The boys I bought the ball for are all under 10.
8. The lady that we work for is Ms. Penn.
   The lady we work for is Ms. Penn.
9. The thief that the police caught was the wrong man.
   The thief the police caught was the wrong man.
10. The cousin that I got the book from is in Europe.
    The cousin I got the book from is in Europe.

17·4   *The following are some sample answers:*
1. Our relatives that speak English enjoy American movies.
   Other relatives do not speak English.
   Our relatives, who speak English, enjoy American movies.
2. The landlord that owns the building now is Mr. Green.
   Another landlord owned the building previously.
   The landlord, who owns the building now, is Mr. Green.
3. Three buildings that stand on Center Street are 90 years old.
   Other buildings on Center Street are older or newer.
   Three buildings, which stand on Center Street, are 90 years old.

4. The contracts that you signed are the wrong ones.
   There are other contracts that are the right ones.
   The contracts, which you signed, are the wrong ones.
5. My friend that lives in Paris speaks little French.
   But my friend that lives in Montreal speaks French well.
   My friend, who lives in Paris, speaks little French.
6. The map that Jim found looks quite old.
   The map that someone else found looks new.
   The map, which Jim found, looks quite old.
7. The best film that I saw this year was a foreign film.
   The best films I saw in other years were American films.
   The best film, which I saw this year, was a foreign film.
8. The country that she visited recently is Peru.
   She visited several other countries long ago.
   The country, which she visited recently, is Peru.
9. The essay that I wrote for his class is about ancient Rome.
   The essay I wrote for another teacher's class is about global warming.
   The essay, which I wrote for his class, is about ancient Rome.
10. The handsomest actor that she met is Brad Pitt.
    She met other actors who were not so handsome.
    The handsomest actor, whom she met, is Brad Pitt.

18 Coordinating and subordinating conjunctions

18·1 *The following are some sample answers:*
1. it was there that she met her future husband
2. it was difficult to communicate without knowing French
3. No one dared to go for a swim
4. complimented them for their progress
5. will you stay home again
6. he often just used public transportation
7. The moment of impact was a nightmare
8. help with the cleanup
9. Sarah is a bright girl
10. being social was not one of his strengths
11. did I get any guidance in how to approach girls
12. work for a year if the expense is too great
13. Jim is a fanatic about fitness
14. somehow failed to include the Joneses
15. gives lectures on maintaining good health

18·2 1. b   2. a   3. d   4. b   5. b   6. a   7. c   8. d   9. a   10. b

18·3 *The following are some sample answers:*
1. my son was cleaning the basement
2. you don't slow down a little
3. I thought of my parents in Brazil
4. I made certain that I had saved enough money
5. she is very short
6. you have your state driver's license
7. You're going to fail this semester
8. I didn't think I could fall in love
9. my father is recovering from his illness
10. I recently lost my job

18·4 *The following are some sample answers:*
1. As his book suggests, good health comes with good eating habits.
2. As you well know, we are having money problems again.
3. As Robert said, the weather isn't going to stop him from going on a hike.
4. Someone said that I sound like my mother.
5. She loves her brothers and wants to be like them.

18·5　*The following are some sample answers:*

1. I know that you are doing your best.
   I know you are doing your best.
2. Jean wrote that she and her daughter will be staying in Mexico City.
   Jean wrote she and her daughter will be staying in Mexico City.
3. The journalist reported that the tornado had done a lot of damage.
   The journalist reported the tornado had done a lot of damage.
4. Does he know that Uncle William passed away?
   Does he know Uncle William passed away?
5. We all hope that you'll be well very soon.
   We all hope you'll be well very soon.

18·6　*The following are some sample answers:*

1. Because you work so hard, we want to give you a raise.
2. Jack is going to buy a new SUV because he inherited some money.
3. Because the weather has gotten so bad, the children have had to play indoors every day.
4. You got a low grade because you don't spell correctly.
5. Because Mr. Fowler has done such good work, he's going to be promoted to head programmer.

19　Phrasal verbs

19·1
1. Past: Those boys were up to something dangerous.
   Present perfect: Those boys have been up to something dangerous.
   Future: Those boys will be up to something dangerous.
2. Present: We check into our motel around sunset.
   Present perfect: We have checked into our motel around sunset.
   Future: We will check into our motel around sunset.
3. Present: I do the entire assignment over again.
   Past: I did the entire assignment over again.
   Future: I will do the entire assignment over again.
4. Present: Does she figure out the solution?
   Past: Did she figure out the solution?
   Present perfect: Has she figured out the solution?
5. Past: How did you put up with their bickering?
   Present perfect: How have you put up with their bickering?
   Future: How will you put up with their bickering?

19·2　*The following are some sample answers:*
1. out　2. figure　3. do　4. onto　5. check　6. off　7. out　8. put　9. check　10. be

19·3　*The following are some sample answers:*
1. Please fill in each blank.
   Please fill each blank in.
   Please fill it in.
2. I'll fill out the questionnaire.
   I'll fill the questionnaire out.
   I'll fill it out.
3. Don't fill up the tank.
   Don't fill the tank up.
   Don't fill it up.
4. Tim gave away five books.
   Tim gave five books away.
   Tim gave them away.
5. The captain won't give up the ship.
   The captain won't give the ship up.
   The captain won't give it up.

19·4　*The following are some sample answers:*
1. Can you fill in for Mary tonight?
2. I need to give up coffee.
3. I'll never give up on my best friend.

4. John gave in to her and went to the movies.
5. That beam looks like it's about to give out.
6. I never went for classical music.
7. My son goes in for wrestling and boxing.
8. We need to go into the details of your story.
9. She's not sure she can go through with the wedding.
10. I'd really like to go out with your sister.

19·5
1. Try to keep out the tourists a little longer.
   Try to keep them out a little longer.
2. You let the whole family down with your actions.
   You let them down with your actions.
3. It's hard to make out the skyline in this haze.
   It's hard to make it out in this haze.
4. Who made these lies up about the mayor?
   Who made them up about the mayor?
5. You just ran over my foot!
   You just ran over it!
6. Let's run the victory pennant up as we come into the harbor.
   Let's run it up as we come into the harbor.

19·6
The following are some sample answers:
1. Can you keep up with the other runners?
2. Why didn't you let me in on the secret?
3. What do you make of this horrible situation?
4. I ran up against some criminals.
5. We have to keep on trying.
6. I'm going to let you in on a promise I made to my mother years ago.
7. Jim finally made up with his girlfriend.
8. We've run out of money. It's time to go home.
9. I want to make up for any harm I've done.
10. Don't let on that you know about their divorce.

19·7
The following are some sample answers:
1. Someone set off a bomb.
   Someone set a bomb off.
   Someone set it off.
2. They're setting up a fruit stand.
   They're setting a fruit stand up.
   They're setting it up.
3. Can we take in another refugee?
   Can we take another refugee in?
   Can we take him in?
4. Take down her statement.
   Take her statement down.
   Take it down.
5. I turned the thieves in.
   I turned in the thieves.
   I turned them in.
6. Turn up the volume on the radio.
   Turn the volume on the radio up.
   Turn it up.

19·8
The following are some sample answers:
1. Laura tried to set us against one another.
2. The hikers set out for the next town.
3. I'll stand by her through thick and thin.
4. I won't stand for any more of your nonsense.
5. We have to stand up for our rights.
6. She took down the address of the outlet store.
7. Some men took off into the woods.
8. Their daughter has turned into a beautiful woman.

9. We walked up to the door and knocked.
10. How could you walk out on your family?

20 Writing

20·1 *The following are some sample answers:*
1. Our new neighbors come from Italy.
2. Haven't you met our new neighbors yet?
3. We're going shopping with our new neighbors.
4. The condo president sent our new neighbors a letter of welcome.
5. Our new neighbors will be invited to our next party.
6. I would help our new neighbors if I had more time.
7. Where is the package for our new neighbors?
8. Our new neighbors were being driven to the airport by our son.
9. We are being harassed by our new neighbors.
10. My wife gave our new neighbors flowers from our garden.

20·2 *The following are some sample answers:*
1. Your daughter's boyfriend works with my son.
2. My daughter is a bit older than your daughter.
3. Why did you buy your daughter such a big car?
4. I'm a much better person today because of your daughter.
5. Your daughter that lives in Mexico visited my aunt there.
6. Your daughter, who is studying to be a nurse, is quite popular.
7. I want to meet your daughter.
8. Your daughter was supposed to star in the school play.
9. The elderly woman was being helped by your daughter.
10. Your daughter, now married to a wealthy man, will have a wonderful life.

20·3 *The following are some sample answers:*
1. A few mistakes were found in your essay.
2. The young student made more than a few mistakes.
3. The teacher found a few mistakes in his homework.
4. He got a low mark because of a few mistakes.
5. A few mistakes that make this paper hard to read will need to be corrected.
6. He made a few mistakes, which anyone can make.
7. If you only make a few mistakes, you'll do just fine.
8. How have a few mistakes made such a bad impression?
9. The teacher is going over a few mistakes she found in their work.
10. You still have a few lingering mistakes.

20·4 *The following are some sample answers:*
1. One of the students comes from Canada.
2. Tom is taller than one of the students in my class.
3. Maria gave one of the students a few suggestions for the party.
4. Did you get that magazine from one of the students?
5. When I met one of the students, I thought she was a lot older.
6. This is one of the students whose parents are scientists.
7. I photographed one of the students from Brazil.
8. One of the students had to take an entrance exam for college.
9. One of the students was failed by Professor Jones.
10. One of the most gifted students is Laura Kelly.

20·5 *The following are some sample answers:*
1. The weight of this suitcase tells me you've overpacked again.
2. The leather suitcase is a lot nicer than this suitcase.
3. This suitcase that Bill bought is far too large.
4. He threw his dirty clothes into this suitcase.
5. This suitcase, which supposedly belonged to my great-grandfather, was stored in the basement.
6. This suitcase would be perfect for my trip if it were just a little bigger.
7. Jim locked the suitcase.

8. This suitcase should have been thrown out long ago.
9. This suitcase will be sold at the garage sale.
10. This suitcase, lying in the middle of the floor, is a big nuisance.

20·6 *The following are some sample answers:*
1. belonged to my mother's family
2. you will find very interesting
3. was hidden inside an old barrel
4. was stolen from me years ago
5. you can't put up with my behavior
6. you've become so impatient with me
7. you think I'm up to no good
8. you don't want to go out with me anymore
9. take a trip to the mountains
10. rebuild the gazebo in the garden
11. visit our relatives in the city
12. fill up the gas tank and take a long drive
13. I should have spoken politely to the officer
14. we must have misunderstood the judge
15. the accident was the other man's fault
16. we have to pay a heavy fine
17. if I had known that you were in trouble
18. if I had gotten the message
19. if they had let me in on the problem
20. if I had been able to leave the hospital
21. if I had thought the situation was more serious than it is
22. crying and rubbing his knee
23. having heard a sudden screech
24. seeing a stranger come around the corner
25. having found a shiny quarter on the sidewalk

20·7 *The following are some sample answers:*
1. My daughter is still having a difficult time.
2. There's an old western at the Bijou and a comedy at the Palace.
3. I thought I might get them a little music box.
4. No. Your new suit would look better with a blue bow tie.
5. I think you left it in the car again.
6. But they also speak English in Quebec.
7. I hate it. It makes me look fat.
8. You have to see the town square and the harbor.
9. It is, but it takes perfect pictures.
10. Three weeks. And I'll be at the beach every day.
11. No, he's still dating my sister.
12. No, I still have the same old number and the same old phone.
13. All the girls like him because he's such a great football player.
14. I would never do anything so dangerous.
15. It's spring, and the young plants need the water.

20·8 *The following are some sample answers:*
1. Is your wife with you today?
2. She's visiting her relatives in Madrid.
3. I imagine you miss her a lot.
4. Say, isn't your boy in college now?
5. My daughter just enrolled at the junior college.
6. I can't believe that he's old enough to leave home.
7. But that's what life is meant to be.
8. Are you and Mr. Patel going away for the summer?
9. We enjoy our house and our garden.
10. Give my regards to your husband.

20·9 *The following are some sample answers:*
  1. And isn't that her brother with her?
  2. He's visiting from Michigan.
  3. Does he play basketball?
  4. I really love that sport.
  5. But I think I'm great at hockey.
  6. Being short isn't a problem in hockey.
  7. What does she want there?
  8. I would really like to go out with her.
  9. Besides, you're much too young for her.
  10. I really think she likes me.

20·10 *The following are some sample answers:*
  1. How long has it been since you were last here?
  2. Right after that, I started working full time to get some money for school.
  3. Do you find your classes hard?
  4. But studying pays off, and I'm getting good grades.
  5. I hope you go out and have some fun once in a while.
  6. Going out and having fun is expensive, and I don't have a lot of money.
  7. Wouldn't that help?
  8. But I don't have a way of getting around.
  9. I don't drive much anymore.
  10. Thanks for offering the car, but I think I'll use public transportation.
  11. I'm heating up some chicken soup.
  12. I didn't have any breakfast, so I'm hungry.